The Book of Powers

Published by:
Taijitu House Publishing

A.J. Christoph
The Book of Powers:
Practices for Unleashing Your Full Potential
www.TaijituHouse.com

ISBN-13: 978-0692256381 (Taijitu House)
ISBN-10: 0692256385

Taijitu House
www.TaijituHouse.com
taijituhouse@gmail.com

First Edition, 2015

About the Author

AJ is a wizard, comedian, martial artist, and a Marine Corps veteran; he also speaks Chinese and writes books. Since a young age, AJ has churned what he calls "the continuum of change" — he's challenged boundaries, got in a bit of trouble along the way, but he has always laughed it off while attempting to help liberate others from their "the muck of stagnation." He believes his life purpose is to help those who want to help themselves, and to demonstrate that laughter is an important balance when you are uncovering all of the mysteries of the Universe.

"To be open is to be free and being free only comes when one is living within a natural flow, and only if one can gracefully accept life's changes without resistance, but it's always best to face challenges with a big smile."

Meet the author - www.ajchristoph.com

Dedication

I dedicate this book to everyone who is left.

Good luck!

✠ **Book Contents**: ~

Foreword to the Preface:

If you want to unplug from the Matrix, stop what you are doing right now, put down this book, go outside and lie down in the grass, and stare up to the heavens and begin to notice every single detail that is infinity away.

AJ

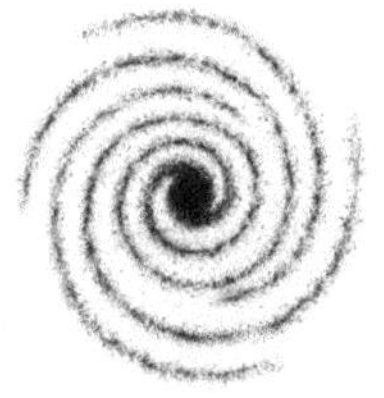

Preface

Bridging the Gap between Ancient Asian Cultures

by Spenser L. Cross

Much of Eastern mystical philosophy is hard to translate into the western culture. This is much of the reasoning behind why Western civilization is only just now, in the last thirty to forty years, springing to life in what we would call "The New Age, New Agers or New Age Thinking." Unfortunately for Westerners there truly is a gap in our learning and Eastern Culture really does have a bit of a head start on us. But needless to say, with some rigorous digging into some digital libraries, we can also find some hidden references into the mysterious ether and other worldly energies even within Pre-Nicaea Christianity, Mystical Judaism, and even Muslim Sufi traditions. But the key is to search for this knowledge in the least expected corners of what most would consider mainstream religions. Due to conspicuous persecution Westerners find themselves in a self-built prison of ignorance stemming back to the death of the great philosopher Hygeia and even before that – the destruction of the Library of Alexandria. But nonetheless, a culture has openly preserved these symbolic sign posts which show us the way to self-empowerment and the rebuilding of the binding energy body.

These Cultures I speak of are the South Asian Cultures. Much of what "New Agers" have been trying their best to define and share with the world has already been documented and practiced in Asia for thousands of years. This is not because they were necessarily the "first to market" with these Self-Empowerment concepts. It is because in their cultures' authorities did not seek to dismantle and eradicate the traditions of Self-Empowerment. They did not obsess over an agenda containing dogma that essentially states that someone else other than you is the only way to soul completion and total Self-Actualization.

The idea of personal empowerment was most definitely preserved in Asia while European cultures succumbed to the Roman Empire's authoritarian rule that then leaked into the Holy Roman Empire and thus finally rests in the Roman Catholic Church and its working subsidiaries. This is not to say that the Christian Tradition is completely "wrong," I am just suggesting that what has been filtered through the minds and pens of Rulers along the historical path sought to canonize an agenda that does not run parallel to the Asian understanding of the human condition. However, once enough digging and seeking has been accomplished in today's digital age, then one with an open mind actually does find many correlations between what Asian cultures know to be true and practical now and what original western traditions, at the time of Christ, practiced and knew then. Some of these practices have been passed down through the aforementioned mystical western traditions, but these perspectives are not discussed out in the open by canonized clergy. These truths are only found when one finds his quiet mind and asks for truth and actively seeks it in waking life.

This truth is discussed in The Book of Powers, by A.J. Christoph. He has put to paper a great translation that bridges the gap between known Ancient Asian traditions and today's western perspective. He does this not because he spends time delving into Western Religions. Christoph does this by simplifying the Asian energy body perspective into a digestible Western viewpoint. Once one reads about the Tao, and is invited to research and meditate on the idea of Qi, then the Western mind is inspired to continue the search for truth. This truth leads to many doors and some of them might be found at your own home.

So enjoy the journey into the Self as you traverse Christoph's work in The Book of Powers.

~ Spencer L Cross, author of ~

THE GREAT PYRAMID: A FACTORY FOR MONO-ATOMIC GOLD

The Book of powers

"Practices for Unleashing Your Full Potential"

A.J. Christoph

Dao

Introduction:

The Disciplines:

The Four Keys to Fulfilling Your Life's Purpose

Introduction

This little book is one of disciplines; energies that will help carry you and your awareness on to the next level. Without discipline your efforts are diluted, futile, and weak. So in order to strengthen your efforts, concentration is required. When you think about it, concentration is a form of discipline, the more concentration that you exert; the higher the probability the event that you desire will come true. This book is an action plan to help assist people in developing discipline, concentration, and an unrelenting dedication. This is a book of truths, wisdoms, visions and realities - it is a "Book of Powers." In one instance it is a channel for success but it is not a rule book. It is simply a guide that will help offer suggestions in locating the keys that will unlock the secrets of your Inner Mystery. This book will help you become aware of your potential, tap into it, and free those brave enough to step up to a higher plane of understanding. However, you have the liberty to take from it what suits you and to omit the things that do not line up with your personal destiny.

The structure of this book follows four broad categories of disciplines: physical discipline, emotional discipline, mental discipline, and flexible discipline. Physical discipline is the act of dedicating yourself to the physical effort required to accomplish your dreams. Physical discipline requires effort, physical activity, and concerted action. It requires a follow through with intention.

Emotional discipline is the valuable art of learning to be a master of your emotions, a true warrior and a silent observer — one that does not allow their "self" to react in a way that is not congruent to their overall life destiny or in a way that does not strategically enhance their current position. Mental discipline is the powerful skill of controlling the thoughts that one allows to manifest within their own mind — mental discipline is the dedication required to obtain "willpower" and learned to use "the laser light of your intention" in a way that is concentrated, refined, efficient and effective. All three of these core disciplines should be applied in a way that leads one to live a balanced, peaceful, and sustainable life — one that allows you to accomplish your life's desires, quickly, quietly, efficiently, effectively and without the emotional toil of struggle.

The final discipline that should be considered while reading this book is the discipline of flexibility. Flexibility is an essential aspect of learning to flow, like water there will always be another boulder, but water slips around without even being aware there was an obstacle. Flexibility allows one to be freely flowing, effortless, and natural. In later chapters I say "ridged things break." So if one can continuously strive to be flexible, essentially you shouldn't break. Flexibility is also true with all of the other core disciplines including physical discipline, so it is encouraged to be able to do splits. OK, let's move on to chapter one, The Familiar Fable of the Sage.

"I am capable, I am Powerful, I am on my way to a different place."

~Nahko Bear

1

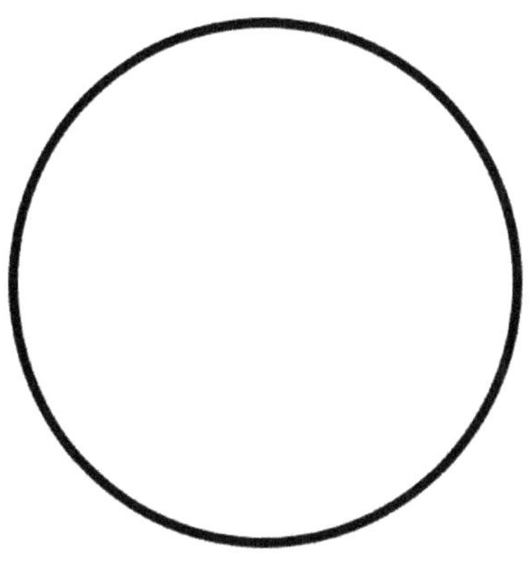

Dao creates one

Chapter 1:

The Familiar Fable of the Sage...

The Familiar Fable of the Sage...

Every so often one crosses paths with a true master. A subtle transaction of energy takes place. There is a mysterious and internal communication that exchanges silently. It is beguiling, enchanting, and empowering. The person is magical and mysterious, warm and inviting. To most people they just can't place their finger exactly on what it is that attracts you to this person, the exact words to explain this subtle feeling are fleeting. It's not a single characteristic, but more so a powerful attraction, a silent charisma that draws you to this person. They act as a magnet pulling in successful relationships, money, love, inspiration, and prosperity. Everything works in perfect harmony for them. Life is easy, they are in the flow, and everything works for them in seemingly perfect harmony.

Although they are successful and exude power, they are usually quiet and humble; consolidated. You may never remember a single boast escaping from their lips; they are secure enough to not need to brag. Controlled and precise, their power is not necessarily that of riches and glamor, but it is more so an immense level of respect and enchantment to where they almost appear to be magical. You could say that they are connected to a higher purpose, removed from the insecurity of the average person. Many people dream of being like them, but very few understand the disciplines that are required to carry them there. Now I am sure you can think of someone who possesses qualities similar to this, and you may have never met a person that is this magical. Just consider the people in your life who possess tidbits of this powerful charisma, and if you do not know anyone like this, use your imagination. They exist but they are few and far between.

From now on we will refer to this mysterious controlled master simply as a Sage. The word Sage comes from ancient Chinese history. The Sages were the teachers of the Tao. (Pronounced Dao but it was mistranslated as Tao, due to the French transcribers not being able to hear the difference.) The Sages traveled the country side teaching people of the ways of the Tao; which is how to live a simple and peaceful life that is in line with nature and removed from the chaos of the human Ego. In Mandarin, Tao has many meanings, but the most basic meaning is simply "path." So the Sages of Ancient China walked the path and instructed others how to do so as well. The Tao is a philosophy that is not so easily understood from book learning, the best way to learn the Tao is to simply sit in the forest at all hours. Observe nature; the serenity of a lake, the peacefulness of a cold winter forest, the refreshing wind blowing through the mountain side, the stillness that is discovered when removed from the world of human activity. The Tao Te Ching, says "the Tao that can be explained is not the eternal Tao."

Now, in the modern day, there are a few real Sages, unlike in the past when one could devote their entire life to simplicity. Modern times require a modified version of the Tao, this physical life usually requires a certain level of effort and activity because we have liabilities, such as rent, phone bills, electric bills, and etc. Back in the olden days a Sage could walk the countryside and simply drift from place to place by living off the land. This could still be possible today, but for the average person the understanding of the Tao needs to be adapted for the modern era. The Tao is eternal, but like the natural world it is constantly evolving, changing, and expanding.

In Taoism there exist a few basic concepts, Wu Wei and the Yin and Yang duality are perhaps the two most fundamental. Wu Wei is the idea of non-action. Wu Wei is the concept for allowing your life to enter into the natural flow. Struggle is not natural, while flow is. If you look at nature, nature does not struggle to survive; only humans do. This is because struggle is an opinion, and only humans have opinions, struggle is an emotion. The grass does not complain and try real hard to grow up, up, and towards the sun. It simply follows its programming and converts sunlight, water, and carbon dioxide into its fuel source. It just simply grows. Similarly, a lion does not struggle to survive either, most of the time when we look at lions and other big cats, what are they doing? They are just lazily lying around, relaxing and enjoying the sunshine, and then, when they are hungry they scruff around for a few minutes and eat whatever creature unfortunately crosses their paths.

We as humans should and can be like that; we have more capability than lions or tigers, but the "thing" that interferes are the evolutionary development of emotions. Now lions and other animals may have emotions such as anger, fear, and etc. But they are basic and rudimentary. Humans on the other hand have much more complex emotions, and often the complexity of the human mind gets in the way of allowing us to be "natural." While everything a human is/does is natural, since we come from the natural world; however, the point being, naturalness in this sense is simplicity — the removal of complications.

Humans are more sophisticated, more complicated, and we like to think we are smarter, because we are more capable in our ability to create. However unfortunately it is our ability to create that creates the complicated emotions that we possess, and oftentimes we place obstacles in our path, and these obstacles prevent us from entering into natural flow. The obstacles most of the time are not real, however they are manifestations of our thoughts, negative yearning, self-doubt, impossibilities, and etc. But who says we have obstacles at all?

Most of the time the obstacles are placed there by other people who lack faith, who lack metaphysical understanding, by people who struggle themselves — so they project their limits onto others. But that is all they are, manifestations of the mind. How many great innovators were told what they were doing would never work? I can think of dozens offhand. Even at one point the top leaders in the computer industry said that no one would want a household personal computer, but how wrong they could have been? Totally wrong. So Wu Wei is the important first concept of action through non-action — to allow your life to flow naturally and without struggle. You still must put forth effort but the key concept is to allow there to be a natural flow in all things that you are doing. Do not try and force anything. If it is beneficial to you, it will happen in its own time without all of the wasted energy trying to convince someone who doesn't wish to be won over. Okay, now let's move on to the next Taoist concept of the duality of the Yin and Yang.

The next concept that is important in understanding Taoism is the duality of the Yin and the Yang. I am sure most of us have heard of Yin/Yang; at a first glance it seems pretty simple; male and female, good and bad, light and dark, but upon deeper reflection one will notice that this duality is an underlying expression for all things in nature, basically everything has a polar opposite and a balance between them. This is the underlying mechanics of physical reality, and it holds true for the metaphysical world as well. For example: masculine and feminine, straight or curvy, hard or soft, tough or timid, big or small, hot and cold, but all of that is still just on the surface level. The two energies as described by the ancient Chinese, Yin and Yang are expressed in everything. When one thinks of a man they think, tough, strong, muscular, hard, dominant, and controlling. While on the other hand, when on thinks of a woman, they think, submissive, soft, sweet, loving, gentle, forgiving, curvy, humble, and free. The Taoist understood that women and men both can possess any combination of Yin and Yang energies, and it does not necessarily have to do with sexuality, but that does play a tiny part of it. Everything in the natural world possesses different levels of Yin and Yang and these terms are just the Taoist's way of defining and describing reality. Scientists would classify it as Acid or Alkaline. Acidity and Alkalinity are the same as Yin and Yang except Acid/Alkaline is specifically described as a property of chemistry. The difference between something that is acidic and something that is alkaline (basic) is the PH balance. Extremes on both ends can kill you. So an extreme of anything is not beneficial to life. This is why the world we live in must be perfectly balanced to sustain life. We live in a miracle world, the third rock from the sun - perfect balance.

Now you can see where the concept of Wu Wei ties together with the Yin and Yang. We strive for balance — this world strives for balance, and when things are off balance, guess what? It either falls apart, or something is introduced to regain proper balance. Below I will show you the Taoist Yin and Yang Symbol with the yin/yang trigrams. A solid line represents Yang energy and a broken line represents Yin energy. Everything can be described with possessing different variations of the two.

The balance within our physical bodies is called homeostasis. Examples of homeostasis include the regulation of temperature and the balance between acidity and alkalinity (pH). It is a process that maintains the stability of the human body's internal environment in response to changes in external conditions. Similarly, the Earth as a planet has homeostasis of its own, when periods of imbalance comes the planet enters into a cataclysm, such as an ice age, or perhaps in the future a nuclear apocalypse brought on by the imbalance of the human Ego. i.e. war. We as creatures of the Earth are susceptible to all of these changes, changes within the Sun's core, changes on the moon, and even changes as far away as other solar systems and galaxies. This is the basis of astrology. At the surface level it may be difficult to see how the stars can affect a person and their personality, but if you dig a little deeper and think about it, everything has an effect on everything else, because everything is intimately interconnected. The separation is only relative to our position and our ability to see and understand.

So this further explains where Yin and Yang comes into play for human peace and simplicity. There is a polarity created between humans and nature. Humans like to think we are separate from nature, but this is a manifestation of the human Ego. It is not the truth. Humans equal Yang energy and Nature is Yin energy. While humans are a part of nature, the human intellect (Ego) is prone to activity, rapid thought, and quick evolutionary change. Everything else in nature evolves slowly over periods of millions of years — while humans, being at a higher vibrational frequency evolve more rapidly. Think about a human compared to a tree. Trees they are moving, but very slowly, they possess a slower vibration of the life force, they exist in a dimension of slow evolution. But also consider this, it is the slow growth of trees that allow them to live for hundreds of years. Humans, being the fastest expression of the life-force on Earth evolve and change much more rapidly; therefore we are destined to have a shorter life. Remember the term growing like a weed? What happens to weeds? They grow real quick and then at the end of the season they die and drop seeds.

If you do not believe in evolution please let me offer fuel for thought: since the year 2000BC until December 17, 1903 the primary method of travel was by the horse and buggy. Then in 1903 the Wright brother successfully however briefly took to the air in flight — the invention of the airplane. Then a few years and some change later in 1908 Henry Ford began the mass production of automobiles. Suddenly there was a quantum leap of human evolution taking place, within the dimension of the human mind. For thousands of years the primary method of travel was via a horse and wheel, then before we knew it we were in the air, and a half century later humans were taking flight to outer space. So if the human mind is evolving rapidly like this, then what is happening at the biological level inside the human mind? Thoughts create change, so there is a biological evolution taking place right now, within your mind reading this. Interesting huh?

The business of a city is very Yang. There is lots of action, commotion, and running about. But if you drive to a nearby forest, suddenly it is the polar opposite. In the serenity of the forest you enter into a Yin state, you enter into a Yin dimension. We generally live in a very Yang male dominated society, and much of our problems are yang problems, they are acidic problems — Imbalance of the Yin and Yang. To provide balance we need less Yang, less heavy metal music, less activity, less fatty foods, more peacefulness, and more gentle relaxing music. We also need less hard liquors and more water. Water is the most revered substance in Taoism, because it always travels to the position that is the lowest. Water is humble. It is no wonder that water is one of the key driving energies of all life on Earth. The Water (Yin) and the solar energy from the Sun (Yang) — these two energies create the Yin and Yang which makes it possible for life on Earth. Other planets in our solar system are off balance, too much Yang, or too much Yin. Both the Yin and the Yang are necessary for the miracle of life to be possible.

Remember with the Yin and Yang comes the alkaline and acid duality of nature. This is basic chemistry. Everything has a PH balance, it is either yin or it is yang. It is either acid or it is alkaline. Now there does exist balance and neutrality, which is why water is so important in sustaining life. It is because of the energy it possesses at some subatomic or molecular level. We are basically made of water; the earth is covered with the stuff. So naturally we need more water. Now getting back to understand what a Sage is…

So when trying to understand a Sage, just think of a person who is in touch with both the yin and the yang properties of Nature. A Sage is a person who is closer to perfect balance than the average person. Most people are off balance and do not realize it. A Sage realizes it and does something about it to cure the imbalances. We as humans are primarily Yang creatures, even women who are usually curvier and more Yin can often express yang characteristics. So Yin and Yang does have to do with sexuality, but it is not completely centered on the sex. However if you consider a macho type guy, what is he? He is very Yang. What will his problems be? Stress, anger, rage, competition, and etc.; now on the other hand if you think of a master martial artist, such as Bruce Lee. What would he be? Bruce Lee's philosophy was to be like water; fluid and flowing (Yin) but can transform instantly to rock hard on impact (Yang). This is one property of water that makes it so dangerous. It is required to keep all life on Earth alive, but if you jump off the Golden Gate Bridge, it will flatten you like a pancake. So to answer the question about Bruce Lee, he was in my opinion, a true Sage. Now I am sure he would have never admitted it, because the moment he did it would not be so. Bruce Lee was a human who was in perfect balance; he was known for only consuming foods/drinks that contributed to his body. He was in perfect shape. He was not big and bulky like body builders strive to be. Body builders are in fact off balance. Don't believe me? Try pushing one over; their bulk, weight, and size becomes a disadvantage in true survival situations. Many body builders are top heavy. What was Bruce Lee? He was a master of the Tao. He understood balance. There was no pushing Bruce Lee over, he had perfect balance. Get it?

Body building is a byproduct of our imbalanced Yang state. A big bulky body builder would never be able to survive for long in nature alone. Someone quick and agile like Bruce Lee would have all of the advantage; simply because he was balanced. So think of life as a balancing act and try to be the Sage and balance your life day by day.

The term Sage is not a religious term. Taoism is not a religion; it is a path of living a balanced and healthy life. There are no rules in Taoism, only methods of understanding ourselves and our place in nature. That is the great thing about Taoism. It is balanced. It provides an understanding of the world without all of the dogma of religious indoctrination. However, many of the great religious teachers of the past were indeed Sages, regardless of their religious affiliation. They helped provide balance at that specific point in time.

The Western culture is familiar with Saints, but the key difference between a Saint and a Sage is; a Sage does not claim to be special or holy. While a Saint is typically elated and regarded as a higher nobler human being, so a saint acknowledges their specialness while a true Sage does not. In other words, Saints are off balance by their very nature. A Sage does not seek to be better than the world. A Sage just wants to understand it. The true Sages of the world are like water, they flow to the lowest position because they know it is actually the highest. True Sages also do not seek observers or admiration because they have evolved beyond the controlling whims of the human Ego.

A Sage is a master of self-control. A Sage is a master of the Tao. A Sage provides balance in every situation they find themselves in. A Sage is one who listens while others speak. One who makes eye contact while others look away, one who looks away when others stare - One who heals others by giving them their focus, their love, and their concentration; a Sage is a master martial artist, but never needs to fight. Because a Sage remains calm when everyone else is frantic — for this reason when other people are experiencing dysfunction, the Sage can provide serenity just by being in the room. A Sage does not infringe upon others, but a true Sage heals others of their imbalances. A true Sage can communicate without saying a word — A Sage can speak without speaking, and can read people without reading. A

Sage walks while everyone else runs. A Sage stands tall while others lean and experience insecurity. A Sage is down to earth while others seek power, status, control, and superiority. It is for these reasons that a Sage is the most powerful, yet the most humble position any person can flow, because he or she places themselves as the lowest, like water, gently resting on the ground cleansing the world. They are at their lowest because their energy has settled down to the point of least resistance; a Sage is totally grounded, and has taken down the Ivory Tower of their human Ego-personality.

At this position on the grass, they can support others and become a source of warmth, light, and strength that other people can rely on, but a true Sage does not seek praise or recognition. A true Sage is powerful, but never demonstrates his/her power — because the moment that they do, the power will be taken away. So a Sage is a human being who straddles both worlds. They are here in the physical dimension, but they are also in the spiritual realms. They have stepped through the gap, and went Through the Hidden Door.

I know it may sound a bit contradictory, but it is these reverse perceptions that enables the Sage to bypass their Ego (Ivory Tower) and place the needs of others above their own. It is a flip of perception that changes one from selfishness to selfless service. It is as simple as striving to make the switch, but before the switch can be made, one must acknowledge their own Ivory Tower. The Ivory Tower is a symbol for the human ego. The shamans of South America call it the madman on the tower or the lunatic on the grass, because the imagined separation between people is an illusion. The higher one climbs up the tower, the more and more ever so slightly mad they become. It is for this reason that the pop-star is usually so moody, for they crave attention and observers. They feed on this attention. It excites them, and it acts as a reinforcing motive to continue climbing. This is why so many people in the media are completely and totally insane. They are off balance. Now this is not to say that one can't be on the television and be perfectly fine, but it can do crazy things to people. The most important thing to consider no matter how wealthy you become, no matter how many observers you have, and no matter how much energy you create; is remember to continuously break down the Ivory Tower. Climb off of your high horse and be grounded. We are all just people, and no one is any more special than anyone else. Specialness is a disease of the mind, a very retched opinion of one's self. So the Sage destroys their Ivory Tower, or most of it at least. It is okay to still keep a brick or two. But the important thing to consider is only keeping the parts that support your life and your goals. The confirming status symbols are often traps that leave you indebted.

In climbing down off of the tower, a Sage acts as a healer and a beacon of inspiration that everyone can learn how to walk the path. They can help bring others down out of their madhouse— The lessons of the Sage may not be anything more than a reassuring word, a pat on the back here, or a silent prayer there. It is not some big show of great power. It is being an in-tune kind and loving individual, and the most magical of healers are the one who never even knew they healed. I am sure you can think of people like this. Someone who just makes you smile from being in the room. But why is this? It is because they exude the silent charisma I have been speaking about. They possess the Silent Power; the unspoken power of self-acceptance and self-love.

It is for this reason that a Sage is a master of self-control, especially in controlling their dialogue with the way they communicate with others. A Sage will always come from a position from below others, rather than speaking down, across, or even through others. Speaking from a position from above can often be interpreted as being combative, and a Sage has no need for conflict; for they are perpetually secure. Conflict is always left at the door; there is no conflict because a Sage maintains no opinions… The less vocal one becomes of their opinions, the less that conflict will occur. So in general try to be the Sage, only voice your opinion when someone asks you for it, and even then choose your words wisely. Just listen to people. Don't try to compete with them. If they want to win, let them win.

In the book Silent Power, by Stuart Wilde, he lays out a thorough understanding of Silent Power. For my purpose of this book I am expanding on much of what he wrote, and integrating my experiences with learning about the Tao. In his book he mentions how trying to be smart, trying to be cool, trying to be noticed and trying to win the approval of others is weak energy, and it robs you of your true self-worth. It makes people feel uncomfortable, it rattles them and they can feel your weakness. It reminds them of their own vulnerabilities and they immediately vote yes, no, or maybe. They resent your weakness because it reminds others of their own insecurities. They will cast you out and you will then go find someone else to lean on, to suck energy from in order to momentarily sustain yourself while you experience dysfunction. So emotional leaning does the complete opposite of what you would desire, it pushes people away. He goes on to say the key is playing a game that 99% of the population does not know about. It's called "Stand Straight in Life." Be strong and be courteous of others and resist the urge to lean. So what he was describing is that Silent Power is the discipline of consolidating yourself. Keeping it together and not infringing on others as much as you possibly can; a little leaning on others in a time of need is okay. But only do so in a way that does not zap them of their energy. Don't be an energy vampire. Read people. If they don't want to talk to you, let them go. Don't hold on to them for dear life like a sinking life raft. Don't do that to others, but also don't do that to yourself.

Now learning not to lean can be a little tricky and awkward in the beginning. I know it was for me, because it often interferes in your ability to openly communicate with others. So my best advice when you begin to practice standing straight is to remember that you can talk to others as much as you want. Just be aware if they want to talk to you. If you pick up any signal at all that they need to get off the phone, or talk to someone else in the bar or whatever. Let them go. Don't hang on to anyone. Let people go freely.

When dealing with people that you do not know, try to keep your most personal details private. This is not a rule, but a suggestion. Sometimes it's great to go out and talk to people and share your life story, but only if it is welcome and reciprocated. Because more often than not it will be interpreted as being pushy— most things people brag about are boring anyway. Trying to speak of your successes can make others feel attacked because you are trying to convince them you are the better, so the other person has no room to feel empowered. This is a form of leaning. You are imposing yourself upon others, in hopes of being noticed.

Let me offer a short story about an interesting experience I had recently. Years ago I studied how to speak Polish. I had some Polish friends in the military and it seemed like a mighty complicated language to learn, so I set off to get a basic conversational understanding. Until last night I hadn't spoken the language since 2011. So it had been years for me. I was out at a bar and I met several Polish guys who went to the local University. At this point I had been drinking a little bit, so my values of not leaning and being silent were mostly out the window. Once I discovered they were Polish I asked them to speak Polish to me. Now remember, I had not a word thought of the language in about three years. They started rattling on and I couldn't remember anything, until suddenly it hit me! I said "Niebo jest niebieski." Which means the sky is blue. They thought it was hilarious and I started remembering more and more. It was good fun. But the point of this brief little story is: you can talk to people and not learn emotionally. Now if they would have been uncomfortable and not wanted to speak to me and I malingered around that would have been leaning— so the key thing to remember in regards to psychological leaning is "how does this make someone feel?" If your mind spits back "hey its good mate." Keep on a talkin'.

It is important to remember we are here to help support and empower others, but we are also not here to brown nose and kiss ass. People love honesty. That is why comedians are so popular. They tell the truth without coming right out and saying it. So just be honest with yourself, be a comedian and tell the truth, but make people laugh in the process. You don't have to be serious.

In empowering others, this empowers ourselves, if you can learn to consciously make the reverse mental switch and focus on empowering others, people will be magically attracted to you. But it isn't about magically attracting people to you, no, that is not the focus. If you are focusing on trying to gain 'followers" then you are going about it for the wrong reasons.

Friends are a byproduct of being a fun, light hearted and good person. So if you want lots of friends try to be a little less serious, and sometimes it's best to make yourself out to be a bit of a fool. It's fun. Try it. This is one of the simple tricks. Stand strong, don't lean on people, and bring your desires inward. Be the magnet of your desires. But don't lose sight of your purpose, that's to be a good person, who is honest, open, loving, and not so serious.

If you seek power, first learn to control yourself, and once you can sustain that for a while, you can begin concentrating on empowering those around you. Everyone will love you for it, for you are subtly healing them by making them feel better, and voila, there it is, you wake up one day with true and unadulterated power. Which is unconditional love and acceptance, your reward will be the profits of selfless service.

I say empowering others is the true source of power because at one point or another, this is what we all need. In the modern world that we are raised in today often teaches us that the way to win and get ahead in life is by brute force, extreme cleverness, and wit. However, the true victors are the ones who win with love, softness, tenderness, respect, and generosity. It is with these core values that the Sage learns to unconditionally love themselves and the world around them. It has been said that the spiritual journey is only three feet. One foot down from your head to your heart and two feet outward to embrace the person nearest to you. This is a perfect summary of the spiritual journey. Learning to lose Your "Self" and replacing that with love for others.

Here is another reverse perception that will help you replace judgment with unconditional love and understanding: I see the world as perfect with its imperfections, because when you think about it, we live in a perfectly balanced world. The only imperfections are mostly opinions based on human emotion and the contradiction of its opinions; sure the world may not be fair, but it's a miracle that we even exist at all! At any moment a Texas sized meteor could smash into the Earth and instantly wipe out all of humanity. So be grateful. When thinking like this, suddenly the spilled chilly on your dress does not appear to be that big of a deal, now does it? I am sure we all have a similar understanding of the relevance that small setbacks can have in affecting our emotional state, but I feel that it is important to state it overtly because spilled chilly is simply spilled chilly. A punch in the nose is just a punch in the nose. A car wreck is just a car wreck; nothing more and nothing less. Ironically the day that I wrote "a car wreck is just a car wreck," I was parked at a red light and a young woman who was in a hurry tried going around me and slightly misjudged and whacked the back of my car. She then tried to scurry off but was caught in the same red light as I. What did I do? I slowly drove up beside her, smiled, and waved at her. She wouldn't look over at me, but I then just drove away.

So for me, that was a lesson on letting things go, and it makes for a great way to back up what I wrote. So try to discipline yourself to place things into perspective. Is this spilled chilly or is it a brain tumor? Both are just experiences of life, and in the end, death is an inevitable part of being alive. The worst that could happen is we die. That is the absolute worst. We all know we will pass away one day, so let's try to enjoy the experience along the way.

Again, it is learning to switch your mind from the finite to the infinite that uncovers the veil of truth. There may be injustices happening all over the world, but ultimately the world is perfect just the way that the creator (God) made it. The injustices are all here for a reason, and that reason is because we incarnated into the physical plane to learn to overcome this human physical experience. We all have specific lessons to learn that are custom tailored to our own individual lives. There is always something to learn right here and right now. So learn the lesson and move on.

Life was never meant to be a struggle, just a gentle walk down life's path. Similarly titled is the wonderful book by Stuart Wilde, *Life Was Never Meant to Be a Struggle*. In this book he talks about the importance of becoming in touch with your natural self, he says:

> "Does a Tiger struggle to survive? No way. He just has a little sniff under his tiger armpits or does whatever tigers do at breakfast time and heads out."

Struggle is not natural. Struggle is usually an indicator something is wrong. But going deeper than that, struggle as defined by Stuart Wilde: "struggle is effort laced with negative emotions and desperation". One person's struggle can be gentle effort to another. So struggle is basically just an opinion. But what is conflict? Conflict is nothing more than a divergence of opinions. This reinforces the importance of trying to drop as many opinions as you possibly can. I suppose it is near impossible to drop all opinions, but if you can learn to remove as many opinions as possible, you will minimize the opportunities for struggle to enter into your life. Now everyone will always have an opinion and that of course is not the point. The point is to become the least opinionated as you can; to strive for an opinion-less existence. And if you do still have an opinion about a sensitive subject, say a political or religious opinion, there is no law saying that you need to be vocal about it. Silence is the Sage's best friend, because in silence you are at your strongest. So try to remain silent as much as possible. Learn to control your tongue. The wise Sages of the past have much wisdom to offer on the subject.

Quoting Proverbs 17:28 "Even a fool who keeps silent is considered wise; when he closes his lips, he is deemed intelligent". Another word of wisdom from Proverbs 15:1 "A soft answer turns away wrath, but a harsh word stirs up anger."

Controlling your tongue is the only way to win in this life. Why do you think our world leaders are such great public speakers? Because they know how to talk to people and this creates credibility and trust worthiness. Whether they are telling the truth or not is a different story.

Moving back over to the idea of struggle; I cannot forget to mention that sometimes the struggle or conflict that we experience is a consequence of our actions, and often they are lessons we need to learn in order to grow spiritually. So maybe that 2nd DUI is a life learning lesson to teach one to stop driving while completely sloshed! And just maybe the suffering that is happening elsewhere in the world is there because those people all need to learn to overcome the lessons of a harsh environment, such as poverty and restriction. Or perhaps they are all spiritual lessons that we as humanity all need to learn to overcome, to heal it, repair it, and make it right. As said previously, the spiritual journey is only three feet long, and we must reach out to help others and learn how to become sustainable as a global society. But ultimately, people need to learn how to be self-sufficient and self-sustaining. This is the only way to create balance on the planet.

This requires education, but more importantly it requires everyone's basic needs to be met. Once people no longer have to focus on just trying to have their basic needs met such as clean water, food, and shelter, they can then focus on becoming more aware of the world around them. But this will not happen without others interference. One mode of thought is to leave the world alone and let it take care of itself. However I disagree. Because if we leave the world alone, someone else will step in and take over, so there is something that we must do to protect the developing countries, their people, their land and natural resources in order to protect them from exploitation.

So in a nutshell, this is the purpose of this little book, to teach the world how to become a controlled master, to be like a Sage, how to switch from the rampant powerless victim mentality to the rarified, strong, powerful, and spiritually mature perspective of unconditional acceptance of your life, in its entirety, the good, the bad, and the ugly. Secondly it is important to honestly address our past decisions and to accept that each bad decision that we made was a sacred lesson that we needed to experience in order to lead us to where we are today; which is on the verge of embarking on the sacred mystical journey: "Through the Hidden Door."

This sacred-mystical journey that I mention is the same journey of the ancient mystics, the world's great spiritual teachers. It is a journey initiated by a few across history but now as times change and technology advances, people are able to come to a point of deeper understanding much faster. This understanding was not commonly available in the past. Essentially, it is the same sacred journey traveled by Jesus Christ, the redeemer, the path that moves people from the very yang oriented world of Ego, competition, and survival into the world of gentleness, softness, generosity, peace, and respect; the world of the "feminine spirit." It is the process from switching from the Yang to Yin.

We live in a very acidic world, but with the invention of technology it can assist in freeing people's minds if they are searching for the right things. Focus on developing complete and total self-realization and with a little bit of dedication, a dollop of perseverance, and a whole lot of patience we all will begin the process that will help liberate us release from our collective karma (the negative experiences written in history.) Once we let go of all of our past shame, guilt, judgment, and injustices, we can become free. Repent for the injustices you have done to others, forgive others for the crimes done to you, and finally liberate yourself from the sins you have imposed upon yourself: The Three Liberations.

Releasing yourself from the karmic shadow of our ancestors offers a perspective that is infinite and unconditionally loving. Doesn't that sound great? The early American settlers committed genocide on the Native Americans, yes, and it is a sad and unfortunate story. But we all need to let it go to start new, because no one alive today is guilty of those sins. Those are the sins of our fathers. All we can do is forgive our ancestors and come to atonement and realize that we humanity did wrong. Let it go. Please let it go, all versions of these stories, the holocaust, slavery, indigenous genocide, the crusades, and etc. All of it, please let it go and focus on the present, the now, in order to create a better future.

Now what about judgement? I hope this will put it into perspective. Judgment is perhaps the darkest side of humanity. Judgment is what creates separation between peoples, cultures, races, religions, sexualities, and everything in between. However did you know there is only one species? Scientifically, we are only Homo sapiens with titbits of other things mixed in.

> If you are interested in discovering your ancestry, family history, what percentage of each race you are, and etc. Visit 23andme.com they provide DNA analysis.

Regardless of what you believe our origins are, whether you believe in the Adam & Eve story, the Big Bang, or even if you believe the world came out of the ocean on a turtle's back. We are all one. We came from the same Source: "The dust of the Earth." Mother Earth is our creator, but Mother Earth had her creator also, the Sun. And the Sun had its creator as well, Father Universe. But in my perspective our Universe had a creator also, as simple as I can explain it, God. But God is not external to the Universe. God is a part of the Universe. God is the energy of all things. God is infinite and so is our universe infinite. There is no beginning and there is no end. Instead, there are multiple beginnings and multiple endings. Yes, the Earth will die someday, humans along with it. Our star (the sun) will die also, but that is just one grain of sand on the beach. We are a part of this fractal infinity. All the way from the smallest we currently know at string theory, all the way up the astronomical with cosmology. We are all small parts of this infinite puzzle. If you can accept that mind expanding fact, it makes judgment of others all the more difficult.

Deborah Bravant said in her article *Free Your mind: Unplug From the Matrix,* "Judgment is self-superiority. Judgment implies wrongdoing even if there is no wrong doing. The wrongdoing is projected by the one who judged. Judgment is an indicator that love is absent." When we learn to unconditionally love, we cannot judge, because judging implies you know best, or that others are wrong. We may not agree with others actions, but judgment, again, is an opinion. When we start to drop our opinions and judgment of others and the world around us; we begin the quest of the initiate, but only you can complete the journey, to make it all the way to becoming the Sage. It will not be easy and the reality is, many of us may fail. But remember, failing only happens if you completely give up, and if you do fall down, get up, dust off your britches and start the climb again.

And remember, your heart cannot be hardened if you constantly strive for softness…

So to wrap up the Familiar Fable of the Sage, you and only you, have control over your life. Your life can not be lived by anyone else, and that is a fact. Others may try to control and manipulate you, but the initiate is on a sacred quest, one that will help her/him let go of judgment and opinions. Once one becomes dedicated that will be the only path, sure, you can step off it for a while. But ultimately, the realization has already been made. We are divinely capable. We are a part of this creation, and therefore God is a loving part of us.

So show the world what you are capable of, not to prove a point to anyone else, but to become better and realize your full potential. Use your knowledge to contribute to society, to inspire people that they too can heal their lives and become the best they can be. Do it for others, but make it a discipline to not tell anyone of your journey; for it is sacred, it is private, and it is the most powerful in silence. Sure you can share bits and pieces of your life to those who want to hear, but for the most part, keep your most inner you a sacred place that only you know. Share only the outer layers with others and once you are ready you can then speak of this great mystery. You can share your experiences with the world and continue to become more and more a part of the God-Force.

And when you feel your life is becoming monotonous and boring, be flexible enough to allow yourself to change your regimen. Walk a different path for a while, put down the book, experience nature, and be free enough to allow yourself to be renewed. This life is full of birthdays; use each day as an opportunity for renewal.

But relax and have fun, it is not a serious journey; if you are overly serious you have missed the point. Remember to laugh, smile, and waste time when you feel like wasting time. Allow yourself balance and get back to work when the time is right. Life gets easier the more you grow spiritually, and eventually with discipline and perseverance we will know our life's purpose, and if by some odd chance that you do not, you will have grown patient by then and possess the ability to say "I am okay with this. I will continue to enjoy life's journey."

Eventually you will become a teacher in your own way. You will share your knowledge and experiences with others who will appreciate your efforts and you will offer them the valuable keys required to empower others along their journey.

This is my goal: to inspire people to empower themselves, in order to teach others to spread the gift of self-empowerment; for this is the greatest gift that you may offer the world, to help set it free.

2

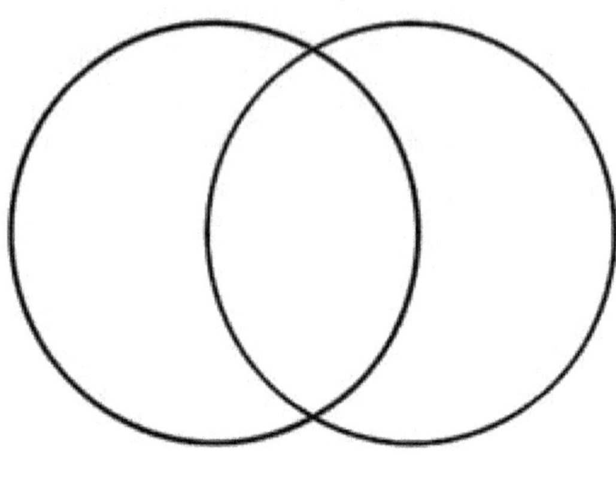

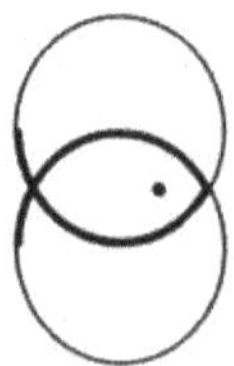

Jesus Fish

One creates two.

Chapter 2:

Understanding True Power

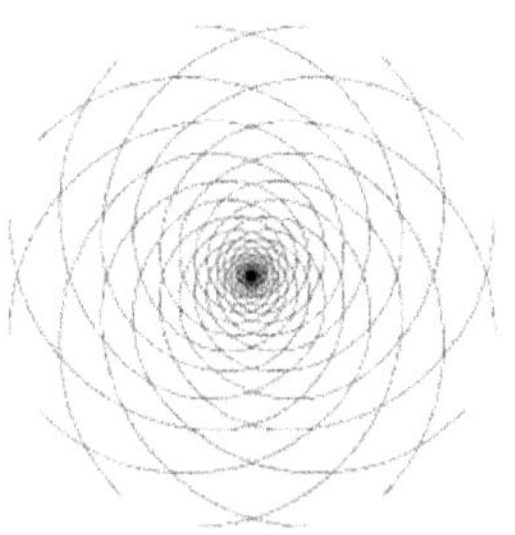

Understanding True Power

Now that you have an understanding of what it means to be a Sage or to be "Sage like," let me describe what I mean by "True Power". I feel that there needs to be a separation between the types of powers available because the word "power" often evokes intense and sometimes very negative emotions; and more often than not these "negative feelings" can create the barrier called judgment and ridicule.

When someone judges something or someone, say a new idea belief or concept, they often shut it out before it has the opportunity to take root to grow into real understanding. This is a protecting mechanism of the mind that ensures the limitation of contradiction. The contradiction of beliefs can make people feel uncomfortable, so to avoid the undesirable emotional response, people shutdown, ridicule, stop listening, attempt to discredit or even quite literally run away. This defense mechanism served its purpose once upon a time in the past, but today as an interconnected global society we need to become emotionally controlled, spiritually mature and sophisticated. One can still have their personal beliefs and opinions but more importantly they should learn to not react out of their emotions.

Reacting emotionally is rarely logical and the reason being, is because since there is no "fact" to support many Because running away from something that is contradiction to your current understanding certainly will become at some point a barrier of its own for real truth and understanding. Essentially this "defense mechanism" created by a conflict with the filter of one's perception, or you could call it the lens that one chooses to view the world through. Notice I underlined chooses, because what you believe is always a choice, it may be values to the core of your being, but we have the free-will to believe what we wish to believe. We have the freewill to see what we wish to see. Everything is a choice.

In the book *The Search for the Hidden Door* by Marshall N. Lever, he describes what he called **"The Religious-Philosophical-Guru Barrier."** This is the barrier created in one's mind that disallows them to move forward out of their current paradigm of thought. I have compared this to a swamp – "the muck of stagnation." It is okay to have beliefs and cling to your faith, but it is also beneficial to put on another lens from time to time, one could call it "walking a mile in someone else's shoes." Before one can obtain "True Power", they must be willing to let go of what is holding them back. One may argue: "I am just fine!" And this may be so, but if you are struggling about your current life situation then you better be prepared to do something about it. **Thought – Word - Action**

The pre-Socratic Greek philosopher Heraclitus of Ephesos was well known for striving for truth and understanding. As far back as 2,500 years ago he compared the understanding of people to that of those asleep. So this need for spiritual "awakening" is something that has been aware by a small group of educated people for thousands of years. Today, I believe it is reaching mainstream to various degrees, but with "awakening" comes one to be willing to accept more responsibility. Heraclitus is also the philosopher known for famously saying: "Change is the only constant." According to him, for one to be a true philosopher one needs to wake up. Similarly, Plato explained the "waking up process" in his story, the Allegory of the Cave, which more or less says that you will never know how beautiful the world outside is until you unchain yourself from whatever is holding you down and make the brave journey to venture into the unknown outside world. It takes courage, bravery, and awareness that an outside world even exists, but once one steps out and sees "reality", they become free. Once one sees there is no way one could go back to living in dark. This is the analogy that the film The Matrix was trying to subtly get across, do you want the red pill or the blue pill? It is always your choice, in the film Morpheus offered Neo the option, but it was his decision to accept the red-pill. He then woke up to reality. Upon waking up he had an enormous responsibility, to essentially save the world from the robots who were living off people's energy, like biological battery power.

So like the Allegory of the Cave by Plato, once one becomes aware of the outside worlds it is their responsibility to come back and offer others the "choice" to come outside and play. But only the individual can choose to unchain themseleves or "take the red-pill".

The red-pill / blue-pill analogy is essentially the same story of "waking up" or choosing to "stay in the dark." The Matrix just tells it in a way that can connect to the minds of people in the modern era. Choosing the "blue-pill" is choosing to go back to sleep and the only reason one would choose the blue-pill is out of fear or the unwillingness to accept a greater responsibility. So basically speaking, fear is what keeps one in the dark or asleep. Darkness can only be banished by light, or better yet, darkness is the absence of light, or even better yet, with philosophizing on the nature of astrophysics; light is a creation from within the darkness of the Universe. This may be a bit abstract but it is true. The entire Universe is essentially darkness and empty space; scientists have titled it "dark-energy". The main source of "visible light" that can be perceived by the human eye is via the billions of stars that scatter the vastness of this great emptiness. All life on Earth is dependent of the Sun's solar energy, and our planet is a creation of our star, the sun. So in a very intimately connected way we are like stars, we are light beings who have the ability within us to cast away all darkness. This is a physical and metaphysical property of reality that is literally the foundation of our creation. We can be the lamp that banishes the darkness of the world. This thought is empowering and helps one realize they can choose to shine their brightest. The Divine Light is the Golden radiant source of "True Power."

In order to escape the cycle of wanting to run back to the safety of darkness, please let me further explain what I mean by The Divine Light. This is the divine spark of life within all living things, inanimate, corporeal, and non-corporeal. If you analyze it from a physics perspective you can intellectually understand that everything is made of matter, matter is made of atoms, atoms are made of protons, neutrons, and electrons. Then zooming in deeper those things are made of what are called quarks with different "flavors", and this brings us to where modern scientific understanding is today, string theory. Stephen Hawking's book: *Black Holes and Baby Universes* and his book *The Universe in a Nutshell* both provide an understanding that the universe is essentially one enormous infinite, for lack of a better word "ball" of energy. It is also mostly empty space, but simultaneously it is completely filled with "energy" that pop in and out of this dimension. To add some further clarity, think of the air that we breath, yes it appears to not be there relative to our size and dimension, but one can feel the effects of the particles brushing your hair on a windy day, additionally this emptiness of air provides the very finite particles of oxygen necessary to breath. What to take away from this is everything is made of something all the way from the negative infinity (string theory) all the way to the positive infinity (cosmology). We will touch on this more in Chapter 4, but for now this image I created will better explain the vastness of infinity; or to phrase it how Stephen King did in his short story, *The Jaunt.* (The Twilight Zone Magazine, 1981)

"Longer than you think, Dad!"

The Positive Infinity to Negative Infinity

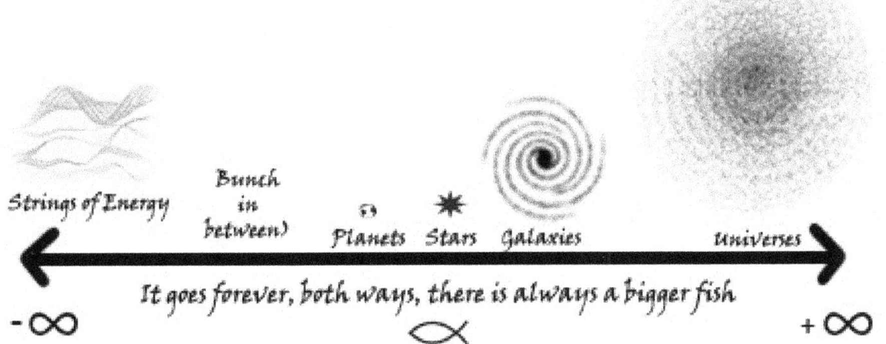

This essence of creation, string theory, energy, or depending on your perspective, you can call it "The God-Force",

God, Christ-Consciousness, the power of God, Qi, Vril Energy, and many different definitions. But all of these "energies" are what creates physical 3D reality, and the same energy is inside of us and can be controlled via humans by the human mind, the clump of organic matter sitting inside your head, your brain, will-power, or to simplify it good ole' discipline & self-control. But it isn't hardly as simple as just thoughts, it is pure intentions, intention comes before the thought or the emotion. So it is just energy, either "high" or "low" energy. But think about it, what else can you control but yourself? For the most part nothing, so that is why I say true power is learning self-control, self-control is expressing the highest form of The God-Force if the intention is pure. The power that makes people feel uncomfortable is the other type of power, which is dominating control over others. This comes from the same source, but from a different intention. That is the 'no-no" kind of power. So with True Power of pure intention and high energy, it is never recommend to try to win, manipulate or force control others because this is an infringement upon freewill. Even in the responsibility of raising children, studies show that an authoritarian rule of does not create happier, healthier, or better children. Instead trust and open communication is recommended, guidance yes, but control no. Just remember the intention is where all power comes from.

The dominating form of control is often the common way, but instead the reverse perception of softness and compassion is the most Divine way. This is the way that the teachers of old tried to teach, Jesus Christ was the bringer of compassion, what did he get in return? Crucifixion, the total opposite - resurrection

True power comes from one place; from within you. True power is not gained by coercive force and it cannot be given to you. Think of this, what happens to many people that win the lottery? They suddenly receive millions and within 6 months, they are either broke or dead. Why? Because they never learned how to manage large amounts of money, so it either quickly leaves them or they die from a money overdose. Self-control is something that has to be learned and cultivated overtime, and the only way to develop it is through discipline, whether it is physical, emotional, mental, or even financial discipline. All real power and self-control comes from within. Now here is the tie in: God is within you. The fabric of our creation is the Divine spark of God. This is why it is important to internalize your concept of God. The old way of thinking was that God is an external, omnipotent, judging, and raging God of emotions. This simply is not so. That version of God was an external manifestation of the male ego, a control power trip. Then some years later Jesus Christ essentially came along and basically said that the old law was bullshit. According to the stories this was not taken well by the current law makers, and so they sent him to be crucified. But for what? For contradicting "The Law." Just because it is written as "Law" does not make anything a moral, spiritual, physical, or even a metaphysical reality, it is just the current paradigm being imposed upon the people based on the current accept or conformed understanding.

In my view, Jesus was an anarchist. He was a freedom fighter in a world that experienced severe restriction, manipulation, and control. This will later be defined in chapter two as "Corrupt Power." But the Sacred Journey of the Initiate or the Sage is a spiritual journey that can be challenging, difficult and even lonely at times, especially if the entire world is against you, what you stand for, and is afraid of change. So this may or may not be our journey as well, depending on each individual's level of courage and bravery, we can all follow the path / the Dao / the way to liberation from restriction. Or we can accept restriction. A certain degree will always exist in this dimension because it is basically a physical law, such as gravity. But when one has courage and strength they climb to the top of the mountain and resist the force of gravity every step of the way. So fighting for freedom is not something for the lazy, it is only for the people who choose to be strong. And the fight is not that of swords and shields, it is the fight to the freedom of accepting responsibility of your life, saying "okay, I am aware I am in control, and if God is going to bless me, I better get off my ass and do something to meet him halfway."

And during your journey of "meeting him halfway", be aware that anytime one challenges the paradigm, there will always be people who have grown comfortable in their routine and they may resist frantically, and maybe even violently with crucifixion. This is the teachings of Jesus: to fight against corruption with the opposite of the enemy's methods, compassion, forgiveness, and understanding.

Our purpose in cultivating True Power is to understand ourselves, others, and the world around us, and then assume the responsibility to pioneer the way of the new paradigm. The new paradigm that is approaching us is "The Singularity". In S. Jason Cunningham's book, *Approaching Singularity: The Genesis of Creation* she points out that we are on the verge of a consciousness explosion. A point to where everyone can now come to a level of understanding that in the past only the great spiritual teachers could achieve. We are coming to an era where humans all across the world will begin to wake up to the reality of the situation and begin to perceive how vast the Universe truly is. Once one can have a feeling of Infinity one will see that the possibilities of existence is much more vast than what we can see within our physical dimensions. But why is that? From what I have gathered, it is simply due to the cycle of our evolution here on Earth. We are a part of this vast creation and as the Universe expands on itself, so do we, our consciousness, understanding, and with that even our technology. But with this expansion comes an enormous responsibility. We can choose to not see what is really happening and continue to "tick-tock" to pay the bills, or we can choose to make the necessary changes within ourselves. Quit literally the survival of our society and humanity depends on ALL HUMANS accepting full, total, and complete responsibility for their actions. If we do not, then we will be destined for another cataclysm like the various cultures in the past.

According to the Mayans, we reached the end of one of the many cycles back in 2012. Everything in existence has a cycle, revolution, period, or "calendar". Depending on the level of dimension the cycles are quicker or slower, we will go into further detail with dimensions in chapter 4 Understanding Dimension, but for now just be aware that all things within this finite physical dimension come to an end. We have the power, authority, and responsibility to either quicken our cycle or slow it down, and depleting all of our Sacred Planet's natural resources will certainly not extend our situation on the planet.

Consider the fact that the Mayans, who were one of the most advanced civilizations known to exist, they are now extinct!

Their calendar was so accurate that it still baffles modern astronomers today, and they even "supposedly" lacked the wondrous gift of electricity, so how did they have such a complex and advanced society? They were intimately connected to nature, Mother Earth, the heavens, planets, stars, and they understood the connections of the cyclical natures of reality. However, that is not to say that they had their supply-chain issues solved - because ultimately they still ended up collapsing in on themselves in their extinction. There is much truth in what they believed and understood of this world. I am not an expert on Mayans or their calendar, but it doesn't take a great visionary to see that the world is changing very rapidly today — faster than it ever has in the recorded history of humanity. So we should take the extinction of our extinct ancestor's civilizations as inspiration to get it right this time around. Things are moving quickly and the laws of physics also apply to the laws of metaphysics. We are building momentum in the form of technology and human consciousness; one of two things can happen. Here are the two options: we either blast off to the stars and find resources to sustain ourselves elsewhere, or we decay and fall back in on ourselves by a lack of energy (natural resources), presumably like the civilizations of the past. Who are not extinct…

To explain this is a more visual way: imagine pushing a shopping cart around Walmart (we call it a buggy where I am from). In the beginning the cart is empty, it is light, and very easy to steer and maneuver around the isles, but as time flows forward you slowly add items to the cart. The buggy becomes heaver, harder to control, and then after two hours in the supermarket you have $500 worth of items. Now imagine that you were not paying attention and you continued to push the buggy faster and faster (demand of consumption). As it picks up speed it also picks up momentum which means it's going to be very difficult to stop all at once. Physically and mathematically speaking, momentum is the conjunction of mass and velocity. So you cannot have momentum without mass (weight) and without velocity (speed.) So as you continue to push the cart up to full speed, you can't slow down, and you end up running past the checkout zone, smashing through the door soaring out into the parking lot into traffic. That is essentially what is happening right now. Time has carried along so far now that we have the momentum of technology, TV, the internet, computers, and all sorts of amazing things. As that technology builds on itself, so does human consciousness. But why? Well it is partly because there are no longer any delays between communication of the world and because it takes "money to make money". So it takes technology to create technology, it takes consciousness to create consciousness, and etc. Today we can hop online or turn on the

TV and instantly see what is happening across the world. (For this reason I also recommend throwing out your TV because it is also a promoter of propaganda, fear, and general garbage.)

Communication of this speed was not possible just a few decades ago. Now with the advent of the internet, we can search for the answers to any question that we seek. If you are searching for wisdom and enlightenment and continuously ask questions and apply concerted action on your journey, our "factual" and "scientific questions can be answered within a matter of moments. Then you stumble across this book, or you find a teacher elsewhere, and the quest has begun. Previously this wasn't possible, people were only fed information that was watered down by the "Powers that be", depending on the location and time period, the ruling power has been the Catholic Church. Information was not freely available like it is today. So the quest for truth, wisdom, and understanding had to be experienced directly or via tradition.

So now the power of self-empowerment is literally at our fingertips, but ultimately it comes from within, it comes from the desire for truth and understanding. And not to mention now in the technological age it is much more difficult to hide things and the truth is easier to expose, it is harder for our world leaders (many of which are corrupt) to hide things from the people. Great example: WikiLeaks. Today mass genocides wouldn't go over very well in a world with camera phones, high-speed internet, and YouTube. People would / will revolt; people are revolting now because we are tired of being lied to about what is really going on in this world. Some people may be at various stages of revolting, but humanity as a whole is subconsciously revolting against "the system" by empowering themselves, educating themselves, and slowly beginning to reconnect to our roots of the Earth.

I am revolting, and more than likely you are too since you are reading this book. I do not want violence, murder, death, or destruction. All that I want is balance and truth. I want racism to stop being promoted on the media, I want innocent people to stop being labeled as criminals for consuming plants such as marijuana, and I believe most importantly I want people to wake up to the fact that we all have unlimited power, and that power starts with your voice. With speaking out against injustice, and acknowledging that YOU HAVE THE POWER! You do. You have unlimited power, but you have to build yourself up to a point to where you can sustain yourself. Sustainability is the key to anything lasting, a relationship, bank account, life, and even the planet. So the revolt is not one of violence and destruction. Wars serve no one any good, it may be a release for the tribal ego of a specific nation, but ultimately the denial of hostility towards each other and understanding the ultimate goal is to balance the Universe. This is my way of True Power. Bringing the power to the people and really mean it, not "we will take care of you, so sit back and relax." Self-empowerment and sustainability is THE way of seeking true power, true power is nothing more than self-control, discipline, and finally action.

The power that the "military-industrial-complex" chooses to exert is the opposite; it is control & power over others. Spreading the venereal disease of lies that we humans are expected to believe that we are weak and have no power, and the most effective tactic is that "to have power is evil". Hurting others is evil, infringing on others is evil, and controlling others is evil. Deep down just become aware that we are infinitely vast, we are a microcosm living within a macrocsom. Once one makes the connection that we are a part of God, you tap into your True Power.

This helps us see that True Power is not a mysterious gift only available to the elite members of the Military-Industrial Complex. It is not the "Divine right" to be wielded over the people; true power is the Divine spark of the God-Force that gives everyone our very breath, and it is openly available to all people to use it how they wish, for better or for worse. For the most part it is neutral and non-judgmental but we have the responsibility to use our power for the betterment of humanity. I don't suppose that we have too, but if you want to be rewarded with the treasures of life, then it is important to lighten your heart - to be capable of balancing your heart between that of a feather. That is our responsibility, not our right. We have no "Rights", rights are the lies created by human law. They serve their purpose, but all that we really have are responsibilities. The responsibility to do the right thing and that is it. This is worth repeating, we have no rights, we only have the responsibility to do the RIGHT thing.

Why do we not have rights? Because "Rights" by their very nature comes from a position of entitlement and demand – "rights" basically say "I am entitled to not accept responsibility for my actions;" which is on the opposite end of the spectrum of being respectful, responsible and spiritually mature. This is what is wrong with many people's mindset today; they feel entitled to a living, to food, to shelter, to income, when many of them have never contributed anything other than plopping out of their mother's womb into existence. I know it is harsh but it is the truth, and the truth doesn't always taste like sugar.

As an example of the demanding nature of "rights": I have the right to go out to a bar, drink as much beer as I wish, get completely sloshed, meet a strange woman, drive her back to my place while being completely sloshed, and then have sex her. No. That is not my right. Yes I have the freewill to do that if I wish, but I am not entitled to do anything just because I live in a free country. So the human Laws serve their purpose and many of them make perfect logical sense, but instead if everyone flipped their perception around and instead viewed it from the perspective of: "I have the responsibility to go out, have a good time, respect those who I encounter, and then drive home safely and responsibly." Many of the world's problems and petty struggle would be solved. No more DUI's, no more pregnant single moms who struggle to make ends meet, no more spreading of venereal disease to unsuspecting people, no more abortions, no more bar fights, and the list goes on and on.

As an aside, I do want to note that my incarnation into this realm was the result of sex out of wedlock, so I am not judging others and their actions; I actually am thankful and grateful to be here. So from one perspective everything happens for a reason, whether that reason is for destiny or a sacred life lesson (not a mistake). We are not the judges of right and wrong, we can't be, because we don't know the entire story. All that we can do as humans is strive to make the right decisions and if a decision results in a situation that is not of the highest energy, then learn to unconditionally accept full responsibility and do the right thing. It can be tough and I don't believe it is meant to be easy. It is essentially the Sacred Journey of the physical experience of life. We come to this world as a pure clean little baby, experience hardship, injustice, and we then make the choice of which side we will serve. If we get the message, we evolve on to the next realm. If we don't get the message, here comes the dung beetle to wash us out of existence. So try not to be condescending, judgmental or ghoulish. The ghouls get the dung beetle.

However, I must acknowledge that a major contribution to one's situation in life is intimately connected to the level of responsibility that their parents assumed. Good mom, good dad, teach responsibility = higher vibration of child's wave-form.

Irresponsible mom + irresponsible dad = a child who does not have many of the keys to success. The child can grow up and learn the lessons on their own through the school of hard knox, but high energy yields high energy. Low energy cancels out the human life-wave.

Responsibility is the wisdom passed down. Punishment and positive reinforcement are the methods of communication when used with compassion and understanding. And most teachings of real value come directly through personal experience. All that one can really share is either a lie or their experience.

> "A smart person learns from their mistakes, but a wise person learns from the mistakes of others."

So in accepting responsibility for your life and life actions, many problems can be avoided, struggle can dissolve away, and life will flow much easier than for someone who is on a lower oscillation of energy. Then the only power available to others who may wish to control you is virtually minimized to zero, because you will be more powerful than them spiritually, physically, and mentally. Their efforts will not work. So all of the disciplines tie together to create a truly "God-Like" being and there is absolutely nothing wrong with striving to be "God-Like". It is essentially the desire to be pure, wholesome, responsible, and clean. Nothing wrong with that, not at all. Those that say otherwise are of the enemy, they want control over you by weakening humanity to a level that is easier to control. But do not become corrupt with being "God-Like", any public display of your "specialness" is certainly a lie and not a true intention. So this is why I speak about in a later chapter the importance of "Silent Power."

So "Power" is not only available to the controllers of the world such as the military, industrial, political, and religious conglomerates. Many people may think that and the "Fat Controllers" of this world may like us to believe it as fact, but in truth, that is slavery and indentured servitude to "The Matrix." The people who seek control over others have a very hard life, it is easy to see, they drive fast cars, big trucks, slave away trying to gain power, money, and status, all to have their wife die once their castle is completed. I really have compassion and sympathy for the people like this, and I apologize if I seem a bit harsh, but in order to get the message across that we don't need all of this crap I have to speak the way that it needs to be spoken.

Chip away your Ivory Tower little by little and you become free! Let go of some prized possessions and try and require as little as possible, if all of humanity required little to nothing then we would be brought to balance and sustainability. I keep repeating these words, because they are very important. It is balance and sustainability that promotes wisdom, freedom, and happiness.

Fear is a program of slavery by the people who wish to control and it is slavery to the systems of control that the "controllers" created. So the "great rulers" of the world are slaves themselves. It is a high stress lifestyle, always cracking the whip of the laborers. What I want to help the world see most is we are <u>all</u> gifted a pure, true, and unlimited power from God. But first we must internalize "God" and bring the feeling of infinite capability inwards, inside ourselves, and then truly believe we have a purpose to better the Universe. We don't have to control anyone but ourselves, and any change we make within ourselves is an immediate and direct change to the world around us. We can't infringe upon people's freewill as that would be corrupt power, so if we focus on building ourselves up, becoming independent, responsible, and sustainable, then we can begin to focus on helping those around us. If one is not financially free, then how can they possibly make a difference in someone else's financial position? We can't just give money away to people because that goes back to assisting the "entitlement" mentality, instead teach others how to be responsible in all areas. That will really do others justice. That is what a true friend would do.

Speaking on internalizing "God", please consider this: what use is a God that is not inside of you? Nothing; a God that is outside is where the idea of the bearded man floating around in outer space comes from. We all know there is something wrong with this idea, but it is what we have been taught all of our lives, and in many religions to question it is a sin. The controlling "powers" of the world don't want us to be free; they want us to be loyal servants and good workers. And good workers simply obey orders, continue with output, and always strive to increase efficiency. But when one makes the reverse flip of perception and suddenly God is within and not outside being prayed too, you suddenly have immense power. Along with the immense power one also becomes aware of the responsibility of such power. But the idea of an external God truly is a conspiracy created a long time ago by "The Powers that Be." They did not want people finding God in their own way because they had a financial institution built, they had an empire, and it was in their best interest to convince the people to confess their sins to the priests, and in turn quite literally hand over all of their power. It is perverted, it is corrupted, and it is a lie. God is within you, but only if you strive for purity, honesty, and truth.

The cycle of the sin confessing worker was created by the ever growing demands of consumption, security of tribal peoples, and the growth of past empires. It was used to further extremes in past days, but it still exists in the present day. Thankfully today people are waking up and seeing that this whole confessing our sins to a "holy man" in a box just doesn't make any sense. Now as a counter point, it is important to confess your wrong doings and the injustices you have imposed upon yourself, others, and others have imposed upon you. But a third party is not necessary, just unless it is a friend who you feel comfortable confiding your wrong doings in. But for the most part release all of your "sins" back into the ground. Mother Earth has far more power to cleanse you than an exalted holy man. The Earth is our Mother, men are often our controllers.

Baptism is symbolic of cleansing, so I do suggest people get baptized if they wish. This is a powerful ritual that shouldn't be over looked, and who is to say you can't baptize yourself every night in the shower? It holds the same meaning and much

more value if it becomes a sacred nightly ritual. Every night you shower you can tell yourself that you are cleansed of your injustices, but make it Sacred. That's what is most important, is that you mean it and will stop doing the things that you know are wrong.

So the only way out of this trap is by taking back and reclaiming your power as an individual. If you are a boss and have to tell other people what to do, try coming from a position of compassion as opposed from a position of authority, either by empowering the individual workers or by us as a society controlling the amounts we consume. If we didn't require as much there would be a lot less demand to make the hard headed knuckle head do what he is supposed to be doing in the first place, but this is a long term goal; something that may take decades to accomplish. And this requires a global strategy that strives towards sustainability. Since all I can do is help the individual, I want you to say: "I have the power. I have the power!" Say it out loud. Say it every day, quietly say it when you are sitting at work, or think it silently the next time you are being harassed by a condescending "superior", say a "boss" or "leader". Another positive affirmation I have learned to regain my power is to understand that I do not have a "boss", even when I worked for a company I refused to refer to my leader as my "boss", but instead I would call them "my employer". This removed me from a position of weakness to a position of controlled strength and power. So say it. Affirm it into reality.

I HAVE THE POWER!

It may feel weird if this is a new concept. The reason being is because we are usually taught that we don't have any power and if we are taught we have power, it is external to us, or it isn't that strong. That simply is not true. You have the power to increase your vibrational frequency through affirmation, education, and understanding. Also discipline yourself to engage in activities that add to your energy, not deduct from it.

We are typically taught that we are powerless and the world is a bloody dangerous place. Yeah, it's dangerous but that's kinda' the point. You are going to die. So die with honor.

Q: "My God! You want to move to Taiwan? What if the plane crashes?"

A: Then I will die.

Q: "What if you get your leg cut off?"

A: I will just kinda hop around.

Q: "What if you go blind?"

A: Then I will hop around in the dark.

It's simple. Be brave, be courageous, be compassionate, and ignore the emotions and fear of others. Everyone will try and convince you to support them in one way or another, that is what people's ego needs to feel justified, real, and secure. Don't let people's weak energy bring you down. Be strong and consider: What's the worst that can happen? I will tell you. The worst that can possibly happen is you die. That is it. To die.

However, death is no biggie if you have a light heart, balanced, and if you know deep down inside you that you strive for truth, honesty, purity, and have previously released all of your injustices. So ask for forgiveness, forgive yourself. Make the Sacred vow to daily consciously strive to raise your consciousness, understanding and awareness. That way when you do finally depart from this physical world, you will know you will be okay – because you will have dealt with all of your baggage when you were living. And also, you are already protected in the first place, all of the fear and emotions are just programming projected onto you by others, they aren't yours, they don't belong to you in the first place, so give it all back!

Then at the moment of your death you will be able to sustain yourself in the next realm, because your energy will be pure, strong, rarified, and closer to divinity. You are what you are the moment you die, death bed repentance and realizations have little value in the afterlife. So it is important to fix your

Life-Wave early on and strive to be as pure as you possible can be right now, right this minute. There is always something to learn right here and right now. That is another spiritual, physical, and metaphysical reality, your life is only a collection of experiences and you have the power to choose which experiences you need in order to spiritually evolve. Some experiences are high energy and some are of low, but the decision into action is ALWAYS yours. You are not guilty of thoughts, thoughts can be imposed upon you without your permission, when we die, we are only guilty of the things that we acted upon. For example: say you had the thought "I'm going to throw this rock through this guy's window and steal his stereo." But then you had a change of heart, you didn't do it. So you are not guilty. But in the physical world of human law and judgement, you would be considered guilty if you "attempted" to murder someone. At your death and day of judgement, you would not be found guilty of murder, only the injustices of inflicting physical harm onto another.

The laws of people exist for a reason, they help maintain order and keep things flowing in a logical manner, but the laws of judgement upon death are not quite the same. You are only guilty of the crimes that you actually commit. Another example, say you had the thought: "I am going to rape this woman." Then you proceed and do it, and in the process you also give her an

STD, she gets pregnant, and sometime down the line she dies of cervical cancer due to the STD that was forced upon her, the child grows up without a father or mother and ends up becoming another Charles Manson. What would you be guilty of then? You would be guilty of murder, rape, child neglect, avoiding responsibility, and diminishing the power of the human species / Wave-Form. So consequences need to be weighed on every decision, but you are only guilty in the spiritual realm if you actually commit the crime and follow through with action. So guard your thoughts closely. Be ever vigilant and strive to become a powerful, responsible, person who conducts themselves Sacredly.

This system exists and there isn't really much that we can do about it asides from controlling our influence to this world. We shouldn't try and tear down the system and the system does help many people get through their lives, because people find security in its structure. That's why it was created, however; the entire "thing" is a holographic illusion. The security that the system provides is not real. Think of how many investors have killed themselves by the emotional whims of the stock market. So what? A number in cyber space fell six decimal places. It's not even real in the first place. It's just a place holder representing something that doesn't even exist. Pretty strange huh?

Money is nothing more than human emotion bundled up and stored someplace in cyber space as unit of "action". I know this first hand that money equals human emotion. Without going into too much detail about my previous life choices, I used to be quite the showman, I was always the center of attention, I liked being looked at because it made me feel alive. Essentially it made me into an observable particle. The nature of electricity is both a particle and a wave. When it is observed it is a particle, but when it is flowing it is a wave. Humans are nothing more than very complex wave-forms, so with this understanding I set out to create as many observers as I could generate with the hopes of licensing the videos to TV shows. I created multiple viral videos and the "ridiculous" things that I done got me on various TV shows such as Ridiculousness, Tosh.o, and one video even created enough emotion that a producer of Jimmy Kimmel Live! Called me and invited me and my mother to fly out to Hollywood to be on the show, all expenses paid. "Sweet" I thought. So how did I create so much emotion? Essentially what I done was made a big fool of myself intentionally, but why? So people would call me an idiot and a fool. And it worked! It will always work because that is an underlying mechanism of the dark-side of the human emotional wave. So essentially I was playing the emotions of the people who viewed the videos. I quickly learned that these experiences, while valuable was not what I needed to continue to be involved in, they were a lot of

fun but ultimately they were promoting the ghoulish side of humanity, so I moved on.

But I will tell you a secret that many people do not see. People love to release their demons on others, I know this, I am aware of this, and I am sure mostly everyone else is aware of the "hateful comments and emotions all over YouTube & social media". But unlike some unsuspecting people who unintentionally create a viral video, the actions of others can have a devastating negative effect on their psyche and emotional wellbeing. My military training and shamanic experiences has helped me not take people's emotional projections so personal, so I am protected, forever and for always, because words only have the power that you allow them to have. Easy peasy lemon squeezy.

It is easy to reflect people's emotions once you are aware that all that are "emotional swords" with intention of collapsing your energy. Bam! You are protected too, forever and for always.

The videos that I created were of some pretty ridiculous situations, mostly making a fool of myself intentionally so people could laugh at me. But why does this have so much power? Simple, everyone loves to laugh at the idiot, and especially if they believe that it is REAL! What was the Universe's response? I got paid for my efforts. It is called "**creating the emotional wave**

and selling it." If you can create a video that creates enough of an emotional reaction, then TV shows will pay you money to air it on their shows. It is genius, it is easy, and it is free money, you just have to be willing to be the laughing stock, the public jester. It requires you to be secure in yourself and also accept the consequences of public humiliation, which is something I promote. People need to lighten up. Act a fool sometimes. It is healthy. But as I said it is not real, it was the illusion of an idiot that people were laughing at, it wasn't me. It was a character that I created and projected as real. It is with creating the illusion where the magic comes into play, both black magic and white magic. So if you do this be cautious. But pure intentions deliver pure results, enough said on that.

This entire universe is an illusion; it's a hologram that is only real because it is being observed. This may be a little farfetched but I have some examples that will help clarify what I mean. An ancient Taoist teaching is to try looking at the gaps between the leaves on trees. When one draws a tree, they include the gaps of the tree as part of the tree, but no, that's incorrect, the gaps are actually the absence of the tree. The spaces are where the tree is not. So there is an illusion of what a tree factually is. In just a moment I will further punch holes in your perception of what a tree is and what it is not.

So what is a tree? I bet you think this is a tree?

It looks like a tree, at least it looks like what some artist thought a tree should appear to be, but assuming that this was a realistic colored exact drawing of a tree, it would only be half right, only a partial truth. And I will show you why.

That is only half of a tree. There is an entire section of the tree that exists in a dimension that is not perceived normally by the human eye, this dimension is actually impossible to perceive with the human eye, because it is covered in dirt underground. The only way to perceive the totality of a tree of how it actually is to either dig up all of the roots, or use your perception to draw it your mind's eye, your third eye - your eye of perception, the eye of your imagination, which is consciousness, visualization, and awareness combined with accurate understanding.

This is what a tree actually is:

This is where the saying of "as above, so below" comes from. So what many people think a tree is only a fraction of the truth. I think it would be safe to say only a fraction of a fraction

of a fraction of a fraction, because this universe is infinitely complex, and we take for granted what we can see. This is a mistake, it is a short coming, so expand your awareness and you will begin to see what reality truly is. This is wisdom; this is the root of True Power.

So hopefully now you can see a little more clearly how we live in a world of illusions, a world of perceptions, and just because we perceive something as a certain does not mean that is accurate at all. Most things are manifestations of opinions, how we think things should be, how a house should be built, how a car should be designed. These are all opinions that are subject to change at any moment. So it is the illusion of stability that keeps people locked in the matrix, yes stable income is important for being a responsible adult, but it are the ridged definitions of where money can come from is what really holds people within the system. Nothing is truly stable. Even at the atomic level the atoms inside our bodies, world, universe, and etc. could suddenly become unstable and all of existence could literally be erased out of existence, has it happened before? I don't know. Can it happen? Yes, anything is possible, and I quite literally mean anything. Is it possible within this dimension? Now that is a question that will be later answered in chapter 4. But in short, certain laws of physics have been observed and we can be thankful that "The Creator" knew how to be perfectly balance itself when it was never created because it has always existed.

Okay, finally as a wrap up of this first chapter, Understanding True Power, I want to clarify some positive and negative affirmations. Some can heal the resonance of your soul, while others can literally make you sink and decay closer towards death. Be positive and disciplined when thinking. That's the best option.

First I will give an example of some power-debilitating thoughts that I once had. Again these are illusions based on a certain paradigm and understanding of reality that was projected on my in my best interest, but the point remains everything changes. I certainly remember my family saying "don't get a tattoo or you will never get a job." I remember thinking how

ridiculous that sounds. It didn't sound logical; I have seen countless people have jobs with tattoos. At the time I didn't understand they meant a job that paid enough to support myself and a family. Pshht I thought. I don't want a job! I want to be my own job! I want to get paid just to be me! That was what I was thinking when I was getting my first tattoo at Camp Lejeune North Carolina. I was in the Marine Corps and I wouldn't be a proper Marine without a ton of tattoos. So needless to say, now I am covered in tattoos, some are pretty bizarre to those who just judge them by first glance.

What my family was trying to teach me was "people will judge you." My mentality has always been as long as my will power is stronger than the opponent then it won't matter how I look. I could be folded up lawn chair and still accomplish anything that I desire, but that's only if I continue to believe and have faith in myself. So the point I am trying to get across is don't let people define reality for you, who is to say what they know is truth, no one but you knows what your soul purpose is, and your purpose may be to be a walking coloring book. Just be aware that what my family taught me is true, if I believe that tattoos are limiting to my job possibilities. As a counter note, I also did not get tattoos in places that would communicate I was either crazy or flat out stupid. In other words I didn't get a swastika tattooed on my forehead.

One of my friends had a tattoo on his hand, he done this in spite of the system, to prove that they cannot control him, because he won't allow it. He is a powerful man, not with riches or money, but his will-power. Anyway, he ended up getting arrested and because of his tattoo he was put in the gang unit. So him bucking up against the system by getting a single, small little tattoo had a major emotional reaction out of "The system." It is pretty crazy really, but people pass judgement on each other. I guess you could say, it's what we do as humans. So just be aware that every action will have an equal and opposite reaction. If you are willing to forever be a fighter against the status quo, then go ahead and get the swastika tattooed on your forehead.

But now, me a few years older I have realized that tattoos can reveal too much about one's life, past, and experiences. I want to be more subtle, maybe others don't pay attention, but it is important to guard your inner most self. Keep it Sacred. Don't give away too much information about yourself to others, it devalues you and it exposes your ignorance. It is always best to try and be as still and silent as possible. This is like camouflage, blending in with your surroundings and not putting a big target on your back. So just be aware what you communicate to others, words, tattoos, body language, dress, teeth, haircut, and etc. Know who you are and try and communicate that to your truest.

If you are like me and have many tattoos and don't want to believe that your tattoos will hinder your success, then the trick lies in creativity. Be as creative as you possibly can be, create things of value, books, poems, and paintings, whatever your talent is. Create an idea, an idea you can sell to the people and in turn create your own job. Just remember "You've got the power!" And it's true; you do if you believe you do!

What are some other self-limiting thoughts that you may have had? Can you think of any obstacles you have placed before your path? I know I have come up with many in my teenage years. Another one for me was. "If I don't have six pack abs then I won't be able to get a girlfriend."

Eggghhh wrong! Take a look around. Some of the most beautiful women are with the ugliest of dudes. Why is that? Because while the dude may be a little chunky or even flat-out ugly, in one way or another, he's got the power, and power is one of the most attractive traits a person can possess. Don't judge the situation and question how unfair it is that that ugly slob has a beauty queen. This is emotional and it robs you of your self-worth, it diminishes your true power. Instead, if you do not understand why a beautiful woman would date what is in your "opinion" an ugly man, stop and ask yourself some questions. Positive questions. Reframe your mind set. Instead of asking yourself "why am I such a screw up?" Change the question around and ask your subconscious mind to teach you "How can I be more fun / desirable / beautiful?" Again, it is the reverse perception of the common though that reveals the mysteries of the Universe. What you may believe is ugly, may be completely and totally irresistible to another. Beauty is nothing more than an opinion, but what is most important is the quality of the energy a person exudes. This is usually the true source of beauty, looks has a lot to do with it, because this ties in to discipline of diet, dress, and etc. But all in all, people who are beautiful exude a silent charisma about them that attracts others to them. They have properties that are "magical", it may not be logical, it may not even be emotional, and it is more than likely in the realm of the Etheric – the quality the feelings one exudes. One of the key concepts to take away from this chapter is:

"You are only worth the subtle etheric feelings that you exude."
~Stuart Wilde, Silent Power (1998)

Your self-worth is only energy, a frequency, it's a feeling, a vibration, all of this is combined to create what is called The Mathematical being, but it is a combination of all things. This is why discipline is so important in this life. It is the only thing that we really have, it is what separates the strong from the weak, and I mean this in the most respectable way.

So be strong, be powerful, be aware, and cultivate your infinite power more and more day-by-day. And remember, love is not logical. Love is an emotion, and if you can learn how to "make" someone have emotions for you, they will regardless of your physical appearance, but be careful this can lead to "Corrupt Power". This is why it is important to focus on yourself and being the best that you can be instead of focusing on how to "make" others like you. Again, the reverse perception.

All of these disciplines are also important in closing the gap between you and wealth, abundance, true power, and etc. There is nothing wrong with being wealthy and getting what you want, in fact I encourage people to strive to be financially free, I know that I want this because it is necessary for spiritual development. Now this is not to say that the poor are not spiritual and the rich are super spiritual, but more often that not, what I have experienced and observed, people who are poor do not accept responsibility for their life and life decisions, but instead place the blame elsewhere, and when you ask for them to contribute, they refuse, don't want too help, or flat out ignore the issue at hand. So becoming wealthy is important in creating balance and freedom within your life. Yes one could drop off the grid and not have anything at all, but this would be denying responsibility if they were to desire to have a family in the future. Now there exists another extreme also, the billionaires of the world, these people are often very sad. They have the control of the entire world literally in the palms of their hands, but they do nothing to help people raise their consciousness and to educate themselves, but I suppose as a counter point, you can't help people who won't help themselves.

You hold the key to "YOUR" infinite possibilities, no one else. It would be lovely if someone would come along and drop a million bucks in your lap, but you have to deserve it in the first place, you need to be worth it spiritually, mentally, and physically. This is the quest of raising your consciousness, striving for purity; this is The Search for the Hidden Door.

The Hidden Door that I speak of is not only some mystical place in the Jungle, while it could be. But it also might be right here inside you, down in the depths the dimensions of your consciousness. Without giving away too many of the keys: The Search for The Hidden Door, is the search for finding that door to your Higher Self, to your higher purpose, the break through between you and the Matrix, freedom from others control, and then once it is found, you unlock it, open it and silently say:

"Okay, I am ready to step through to a new way of dealing with life. I am ready to make <u>my life sacred</u>, holy, and true. I am ready to allow the God-Force to move through me,

and to act as a beacon for truth, love, light and enlightenment. I am ready to be a healer in this world. To help heal the hardened hearts of the people who have never experienced true love. I am ready to be the warm embrace that will reconnect someone back to God. But above all, I am ready to let go of my injustices. I am ready to forgive myself. I am ready to forgive others, and I am ready to forgive myself for all of the injustices I have inflicted upon this world. I am ready to be free."

Then you step through…

The Trinity

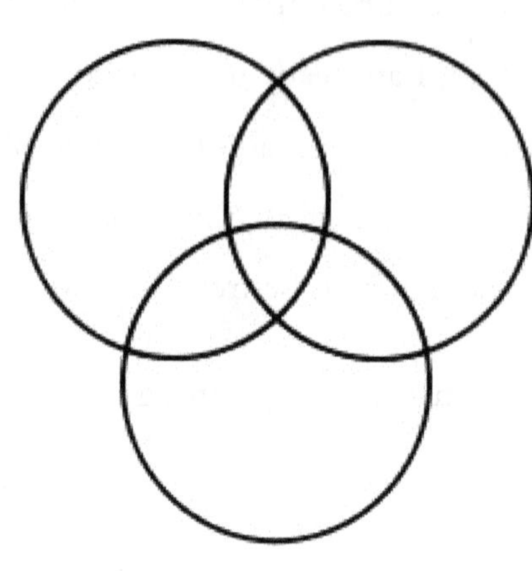

三

Two creates three.

Chapter 3

Understanding Corrupt Power

The Ivory Tower

Corrupt Power

So now we get to talk about the spooky stuff; the stuff that makes people cringe when you say the word power. It isn't pleasant but you need to know all about it. This will protect you from the ghouls, people who are nasty, evil, and essentially want to dominate you. Whether that is financially, mentally, spiritually, sexually, or physically, awareness is always a reliable ally.

Corrupt power, simply put is elitism and control over others. Corrupt power stems from the human ego-personality who needs to be observed to feel real, more special, and separated from all of the peons down on the ground. But of course, like everything else, it is a lie, it's an illusion, it also is not real. The Ivory Tower is the elevation of specialness that makes one act in funny ways. The Ivory Tower zaps electricity of observers, admirers, and this further solidifies that it factually is superior, higher, exalted, holier, and somehow "closer to God." But the height is an illusion, it is not real, the tower that one builds is only in their minds, if you were to encounter someone with a humongous Ivory Tower guess where they would be? Standing on the same level as you and I, no taller, no holier, no closer to God, they are just people with an inflated perception of themselves and it is quite sad really.

The separation of others is created by the confirming symbols of one's specialness, but in reality we are all on the same level, right here on the ground. We might not be on the same level consciously, financially, or as in power status, but ultimately all of that is an illusion. With the exception of spiritual height, that part is real, but I will tell you that heaven certainly isn't up. Heaven is sideways. Not held over the heads of the "unspiritual peons."

Why is heaven sideways? Because it exists in a different dimension, it can't be up, because up is in reference to status over people, bosses, top dogs, the chain of command. To further explain the whole sideways deal, when you flip out of this dimension you actually aren't going anywhere. Why? Because the universe is infinite, therefore every single point in space is at the center. Up is a human thing, sideways is a spiritual thing. And sideways isn't even totally accurate, it is just to make the point that there illusion of height is only a matter of the human mind, it is an opinion one agrees upon themselves or of others. It doesn't mean that it is real. It's not. It's BS.

The shamans of South America called it the lunatic on the grass, meaning that one who believes that they are higher than others are in reality just crazy people running about on the ground. I am sure we have all seen this, and maybe we even have bits and pieces of this that we still need to deal with. There is nothing wrong with having "things" that benefit you and your life, say a nice car, expensive boat, nice house and etc. But more often than not these "confirming symbols" are actually financial obligations. They are the barbed wire of the Matrix, they only exist because one believes that these things are necessary for survival, when in fact we don't really need much of anything. Food, water, warmth, and people to love us and care for us are what is most important. Glitzy shiny things just help keep us as powerless victims in a system that is designed to keep us in one place. Like the muck of a swamp, at first you may feel you are about to drown, but then your shoe slips loose and then your foot plops right out of the gook. The next thing that you know, you are on dry ground thinking "man if I would have just ditched those expensive shoes a long time ago I could have been running around freely."

So ditch the things that hold you back, save your money, spend it wisely, and strive to become more and more free! Controlling others is perverted in a sense, because people usually derive some sort of sexual power out of it. Sex is intimately related to power trips, because the perception of power is the most attractive characteristics in a mate. That is why people gawk over the revealing pop-stars and movie stars, but the real issue of corrupt power is when one believes that they truly are superior and take advantage of the power that they do have over others. This is the dark-side of humanity. It is nasty, it is ghoulish, too put it simply it is "Dominion." In the book *The Children of R* by Chime 1.3.0 he goes into greater detail of corruption, what he calls the "Dominion." The Dominion is another word to explain the ghoulish side of people, but he expands upon it in much more detail. He takes it through other dimensions and even to extraterrestrial control of humanity. I highly suggest you read that book; he is spot on and does not pull any punches when it comes to exposing corruption and "how deep the rabbit hole goes."

I must directly acknowledge that not every human is created equal, to believe this is a lie. It is "Dominion" propaganda, but it is true that all humans have unlimited potential. One may have to overcome more obstacles and it may be a bit more difficult and slower perhaps, but we are not on an equal playing field, and the "Four Keys" will assist anyone seeking to step out of the swamp. Higher planes of consciousness exist, but they are not really higher, as I have said they are sideways, or more accurately just faster vibrations of the human mind. A "higher" energy or one could call it a "quicker" oscillation of the human life-wave.

So what exactly is corrupt power? Corrupt power is low energy; it is the muck of the swamp, the opposite of freedom. Corrupt power is all of the power that seeks to control, entrap, ensnare, indebt, and restrict people and limit freewill. The world is full of it. I am sure you already know a lot of it. This type of power is usually only pleasing in terms of power over others; such as military, religious, and social power, the power that is pleasing to the human ego. The part of your personality that likes to be observed, recognized, and feel "special." It is important to say again, specialness is another dark-side of humanity, because it creates separation, "us and them", much like judgment. Judgment and specialness both go hand-in-hand. You can't have one without the other. We should remove judgment and instead move towards high energy and away from low energy. Not that we are any more special, better, or holy, but because as they say "birds of a feather flock together." Either you will raise their energy or they will bring you down. This is especially true with drug addiction, if you are stepping away from drug addition, it would not be smart to hang around crack houses or you fall and decay right back to where you were.

Our world is dominated by the power of specialness, fast cars, big houses, expensive shoes, and all of that. They are usually all forms of entrapment. But to add further clarity how these forms of corrupt power can take hold in people's lives I will offer some financial examples. In the book *Rich Dad Poor Dad* by Robert Kiyosaki and Sharon Lechter, they talk about how poor people mistake liabilities as assets. In other words they get basic accounting backwards. Many people think that their house is their biggest asset, but it's not! It is usually your biggest liability; especially if you don't really own the house. If you took out a 30 year mortgage out on your house, then that house does not belong to you. It belongs to the bank. So you are spending thousands of dollars per-year just to pay off the interest. You aren't even paying for the house until you have some equity built up. So to shorten all of this: assets put money in your pocket and liabilities remove money.

Writing a book with the intentions of selling it is creating a capital good. Capital goods are things such as tractors, computers, shovels, cameras and etc. Anything that can be used to generate revenue. A true investment is something that will put money in your pocket without you having to tend to it. If you start a business that requires you to go to work every day, that is not an investment, that's a job. Jobs swap hours for dollars, investments generate revenue without having to do anything further provided the time and energy put in is enough to sustain itself. So a book becomes an asset only when and if it starts selling. That is the key to freeing yourself from the financial control of the Matrix, you have to learn to use your creativity to generate additional streams of income, this way you are <u>free</u> to spend your time elsewhere. So investing in houses, cars, and jewelry are all liabilities if you have to make payments on them.

Now if you bought a small house with cash up-front, and started running a business out of it, it would then become an asset, but only if it is assisting in putting money in your pocket. Some people buy real estate, fix it up, and then swap it for cash, this is an investment but you are at the whims of the property market, creating items such as book and music hold more value because it is not a onetime sell. It is something that one can sell for the rest of their lives. So now that you have a basic understanding of investments, capital goods, and liabilities you know that assets put money in and liabilities take money away.

So the tie together to the dark-side of "Corrupt Power" is with the people who want to trick us into making a decision that is not truly in our best interest. Also known as debt, or more directly put disguised slavery. How does that happen? More often than not, simply by a lack of understanding of the marketplace combined with some dark-side power trickery. One could phrase it as:

"Buy this house and become a worker for the bank!"

or

"Take out this loan and become a worker for the government!

Corrupt power is the conscious manipulation of people to get something that will benefit you at their expense.

Convincing the little old couple to sell their thirty ounces of Gold for $20,000 and then making $76,000 profit off of them and their ignorance of the current market price, not good. Corrupt Power is taking advantage of people, while smooth talking them into decisions that are not in their best interest.

Sometimes corrupt power can even be a decision inflicted upon yourself. For what? For something that has tricked you into needing it, AKA marketing of a piece of junk product that does not do what it claims. They are taking advantage of people who usually don't know any better. Now I am not saying that the people who use corrupt power are 100% evil people. No they are not completely evil, but the analogy that was used to describe it is they are like spoiled children hoarding up all of the toys. What is the steam of the problem? Basically it is fear. The fear of not having enough. If one is satisfied with what they do have, then the problem solves itself.

In an interview sometime back in the 20th century the Oil Tycoon John D. Rockefeller was asked: "How much is enough?" He replied: "Just a little bit more." So it is the uncontrollable desire for more and consumption that allows corrupt power to manifest. This goes all the way from the micro to the macro, from the abusive partner to the corporations who have no respect for the Sacredness of the Earth. Their eyes are focused on the construction of luxury resorts in the Grand Canyon, but for what? So they can further exploit the planet and increase revenue for their corporation. This is why sustainability and responsibility is so important, without out it we literally are destined to come to destruction. But why? I can't imagine a world without trees being a very hospitable planet. An overrun concrete jungle is hardly balanced enough to support life.

However, in contrast people need a way to purchase their first home, especially if you can't afford it with cash up-front. But the main thing to take away from this is to make it a responsibility to live within your means. Maybe easier said than done, but this is the only way to rebalance this planet and to allow all of humanity to come to a point of consolidation. You have the power remember. So don't let the pushy salesman convince you to make a decision that is not in your best interest. Is it not true that most salespeople have a vested interest in your purchase decision? Of course, it's called commission. They are not evil because they want you to buy the house that will make your hair fall out trying to make the payments. They just want to increase <u>their</u> efficiency and to make the most out of their time and effort. They are not dark people and you are not all bloody white either. We are all just trying to get by within a system that is made to create indebtedness and indentured servitude. It may sound harsh, but quite literally the system is designed to keep people down at a lower level of awareness because they are too busy trying to make ends meet, or alternatively they are too preoccupied with whatever program is currently on the telly. Notice I said program. Why did I say program? Well first off because it is a computer programming that is set to air via radio waves, and secondly, well… That is how people are "programmed." Throw the TV out, or at least watch as little as possible and for short amounts of time. There "ain't" no medicine on the TV, just emotional waves programmed to get people bent all out of whack. Like the addiction of the news, always tuning in for more drama.

Now you may be thinking what about military, social, and religious power? Well what about them? Are they trying to control you? Do they have an agenda that is contradictory to your own? Better believe it. The military believe it or not is actually one of the less corrupted forms out there. I know it may be hard to believe, but it's true. While I don't agree with the political aspects of the military and especially when it comes to meddling in other countries affairs, but the people in the military have real world experience, they know death, and they also know and are even taught how to say with confidence: "This is bullshit."

If the military is the least corrupt, then what is the most corrupt? It won't take long to figure this one out. The most corrupt would have to be the ones disguised as the most "righteous". So the religious organizing bodies who collect billions of dollars per year off 80 year old grannies living alone in their apartments. These TV programs are as ghoulish as they come. They literally use the emotional manipulation to squeeze every last penny out of the elderly's already dusty pocket books.

Not all religious organizations do this, many are truly doing good, and the evil ones still do good deeds, but not near enough to balance their robbery by black magic manipulation. Enough said on them. Be aware, and please, don't send them money. Because it's not going where they say it is. It's going so they can buy another BMW or something. No preacher who is teaching the truths of Christ would need a multimillion dollar mansion. They will pay for it in the end. We don't have to judge them. But when their moment of death comes, they may wish they had chosen a different way of dealing with life. The dung beetle will roll them up and they will be washed out of existence.

Dry, cut, and simple; no true saint would try to control anyone especially by low level manipulation scare tactics. Jesus never tried to control anyone and neither did Buddha or any of the other enlightened teachers. They all promoted freedom from the systems which were corrupt. It doesn't take a great visionary to see who has your best interest in mind. Have a little look around. What are they telling you? Are they saying: "Trust us. We are a good bank?" Well if their marketing strategy is "hey public trust us." Then that certainly means there is a lack of trust that they are trying to compensate for. No way I will trust them, I trust myself, I don't trust any loan, no matter how lucrative it sounds. Because in the end, if you accept anything on credit, you have the responsibility to pay it back. So it is always best to live within your means, and better yet! Make your own bank! Called The Bank of Financial Responsibility! Put more into savings accounts and spend less on things that no one needs.

Now obviously in creating your own bank I am just joking around, but if you run your bank account like a bank operates, then you truly will be better off. How do you do this? The basic thing to know is a bank has what is called a required reserve. This means if someone puts $100 in, they will take something like 30% and put it aside. They do this for all accounts. This acts as security to ensure if someone comes and makes a large cash withdrawal, they will have the cash available to give out.

So try this, it might be difficult, but it is the best advice I learned in business school, try to maintain a 40% required reserve. Anytime you make any money, put 40% into your savings account. Then donate 10% to a cause that you believe in and finally live on 50%. Over the years you will have donated a lot of money to supporting a good cause, you will have much cash on hand, and you will be living well within your means.

Then after some time you can use your cash from your saving account for a big investment and have the opportunity to retire early and not depend on government programs and etc. This is the responsible way of dealing with finances.

And remember to be cautious when dealing with people. People will almost always have ulterior motives than what they admit — especially when it requires a contract and the taking on of debt. In the military we call this not being complacent, the Marine Corps teaches "complacency kills?" Why does it kill? Because if you are not aware and paying attention someone might come by and whack ya! Maybe you will live, maybe you will die, but if you are looking out for yourself and each other, then everyone is better off.

So what about money? Is money good? Bad? Downright evil? Money is neutral; much like how it can be used to build an atomic bomb or used to provide clean water to a village. Money is neutral; the intention behind the money is where the answer lies. You can do good or evil. It is always a choice. We have free will, and it is important to be generous in this life. Being generous is a magical reverse trick that opens one up to receive more. The more you are willing to give of yourself unto others, the more others will be encouraged to give back to you. Profits are the rewards of good service, and people are the custodians of wealth. So be good to people, help when asked, and create an energy about yourself that empowers others. But if you need too, don't be afraid to send an invoice for the bill, otherwise people will skate by without ever paying. So you must learn to ask to be paid. The system is setup to where the "little people" feel uncomfortable asking to be paid. "Excuse me sir, another bowl of slop please." So ask for it and you will get it. Be fair, don't overcharge, but ask what you are worth. Then as your skills increase, increase your prices. No one says poverty is holy. It isn't. Poverty is the biggest injustice one can impose upon themselves, but being greedy is equally hindering in spiritual liberation. Why? The reason is simple; a big heart big money, a little heart a little money.

What is money if it is not true power?

From what I have gathered they are all aspects of power but money is essentially a physical manifestation of ones will-power, concentration, emotions, creativity, and intention. Will Power is also known as "Magick". Magick as defined by the infamous occultist Aleister Crowley is: **"the science and art of manifesting change in conformity with will."**

So basically this type of power is nothing more than the ability to cause change in the world around you, and if you want to change anything it will require money to some degree or another. Now I speak on not infringing and not trying to change the world or save the world and etc. But we are "like Gods" created in "his image." What this means to me is, we have the ability to create and change the world around us, so we need to be conscious of which side that we serve. Essentially are we serving humanity? Or are we further serving the destruction of humanity? It is a tough question to ask oneself because it requires a 100% and totally honest answer. So, first comes the intention, then the thought, then the word and finally the action.

Thought-Word-Action

So the first thing that manifests is one's intention, then their thoughts, and the rest is the byproduct of their creativity and the reactions of their intentions. So it is important to have the right intention behind every thought, if the intention is wrong, then corruption will certainly follow.

Corrupt Power is usually only temporary and is only defined in terms of the feeling that one gets for controlling others, and when you think about it, this is the opposite of true power. Having to control others is another form of entrapment or enslavement. Always having to express control over others is insecure and weak, why would you want to control anyone anyway? Is it not better to be a guide as opposed to being a "ruler" and demonstrate to others how to successfully lead their own lives instead of having to micromanage everyone all of the time? Think of the old industries of the past. Slave drivers, increase output, increase efficiency. But today in the modern world companies such as Starbucks take advice from the ground up. One of their bestselling coffees was actually an idea of a functional level barista. Pretty cool huh? However it's not cool that they pay the farmers pennies to grow the coffee beans and then turn around and sell it to the public at $10 a cup. Paying that much for a cup of coffee is irresponsible to me, but even more irresponsible is the exploitation of the poorest of the poor people at the bottom - the people who provide the raw materials. Now I am not going to get into fairness because we do not live in a fair world, but there is an exploitation of people that exists, and I would not be doing my job if I didn't point it out and expose it. Instead of focusing on "what is best for the company" if they would flip their perception from selfishness to selflessness of "What is best for the Earth / Humanity" they could still grow and survive as a company, and all people along the supply chain would be taken care of. But doing this would put "The Powers the Be" to a position of self-actualization and responsibility. This would also mean that they may not be able to have multi-million dollar yearly bonuses.

So the corrupt version of power is the power of controlling others for some "elite" few's personal benefit. They do not have the Earth or humanity in mind. Corrupt Power is selfishness. But why does it exist in the first place? Repeating a previous statement, not everyone is on an equal playing field, both with intelligence, physique, and social capabilities. So the systems of control were created early on to get the best out of their armies. People back in the olden days needed to band together in order to survive, so it was a survival tactic of humanity. The same as today but it is different - instead of striving to survive as a nation, tribe, state, city, and etc. We need to switch to striving for what is responsible and right for all of the Earth, what is right for all of humanity, we need to get over this "us and them" complex of previous centuries, and we need to focus on removing corruption off the planet. We desperately need balance.

So external control over others is a survival tactic of the human Ego-personality that helps cultivate security, generate wealth, and create an empire. So I suppose you could say power of this nature is in a way the complete opposite of liberating true self-empowerment (internal power), at-least in the modern world But why? Perhaps it is because it is an over compensation for the lack of internal security. In America and elsewhere we live in an independent society, as people we are gaining freedom, but we are intimately connected globally. Most of our consumer products like shoes, shirts, knickknacks, and etc. come from developing countries, while the "quality" related high-tech products are developed in the U.S.A. Yes there are exceptions, but you can see the point, it is all about the wealth of each country, not the overall security of the planet.

We are approaching self-realization as a Global Society. The developing countries are where some major changes are going to occur. Places like the African countries that are literally barely involved in the money markets at all, they are the people who will drastically explode once they enter into the money markets and become "American-Like" consumers. Once their basic needs are met, they will have the liberty to grow intellectually, physically, and spiritually. But what will happen then? Assuming we have the resources to sustain this global expansion, it is hard to tell, but I am not certain our society can handle another 5 billion automobiles consuming more oil and pumping out more pollution. If we can handle it then we will have a major supply crunch for oil, the entire oil industry is a true conspiracy. The sun powers all life, it could power the world, but that wouldn't be very profitable. Free energy does not create empires.

Now I must admit the world has to have its leaders. (Notice I did not say rulers?) People need good leaders. But at the same time the greatest of leaders teach about the ideas of freedom. Freedom is what the world needs, not micro-managing control. Now some areas of the world are not ready for freedom yet, and other areas are. So just consider the world is a coevolving planet and as things change, technology helps with the spreading of wisdom— the dispersion of freedom and the awareness of responsibility.

The areas that are less free are that way because of the lack of communication technology and spiritual / metaphysical understanding and a lack of resources and infrastructure. It also has to do with race and the capacity of certain tribal peoples. Partially they don't want the technology and partially we as a developed technological society find it more beneficial to exploit them as opposed to educate them.

Here communication is the key factor in spreading powerful ideas such as spiritual freedom. Take North Korea for example. It is a nation of slaves, may happy slaves, but the sad thing is they do not have the freedom to even question whether or not they are free. Here in America where I am typing this book, I have the freedom to question my freedom, so this leads me to believe that I truly am free. Are there more free areas elsewhere in the world? Certainly, but freedom is an idea. And as long as the thought has the ability to be had, it has the ability to grow. So water it, tend to it, and don't allow it to become corrupted with the heroine of power. Because you are free does not mean you have the "Rights" to step on those less free. Get it? Got it? Good.

It is important to drop the seeds of freedom into the minds of others, but it is equally important to allow people to make their own decisions no matter how silly they choose to be. A Sage is emotionally removed from the actions of others, while simultaneously being emotionally empathetic of other's needs and situation. People must be given the freedom to make their own decisions and be allowed to spiritually grow accordingly, especially when it comes to who or what to believe. Infringing on others does not do you or others any justice, and it can also create conflict. So the rule of thumb is plant the seed, let it grow, and water it as needed. It is a very Yin method of educating people. Leaders are not to be rulers over others; a leader is more of a gardener. Proper sunlight and water are a must, but if you have ever grown any plants, the first lesson you will learn is if you overwater them you will kill em'. Love is like a gentle rain. Remember to love your flowers and give them only what they need, nothing more, and nothing less.

Only the individual knows what is best for them, and imposing on them suggests that you know better than them. Perhaps their decisions are self-destructive? Then what? How do you know their destiny is not to live a hard life on the streets, only to discover 40 years later they can do better? You can nudge them in the right direction, but the decision will always be theirs. Or as they say, you can lead a horse to water, but you can't make him drink— that's when you beat it into submission and teach em' a good-ole'-fashion life controlling lesson.

This is why what I call "True Power" like a Sage possesses, is quietly and ever so gently expressed, it is the subtle flow of love through you, self-love, and understanding of others. It is the radiating energy of the God-Force that gives you your very breath. In my mode of thought, we call it the etheric life-force. There is something electrical inside our bodies that make our heart beat. If you have a heart attack, what do medical professionals use? A defibrillator; they shock your body back into working electrical order. But what does that mean? Well, to me, it tells me, we are made of light, electrical energy. Light consists of two different things, the particle state called electricity, and the wave state known as magnetism. It is the particle/wave duality, meaning light has both characteristics of a particle and a wave. Or you could say light possess yin and yang qualities, just like everything else.

Once our light leaves our physical body we pass away. But where does the light go? Well it goes back into the Universe. But it was still in the universe to begin with. So it didn't really go anywhere. It just moved on to another location. The 2nd law of thermodynamics says that energy cannot be created nor destroyed. It can only be rearranged. So you have to look at this life as one big system, and we happen to be a part of it. Even when we die, we are still a part of it, just at a different vibration of existence. So I call it the etheric, but you can feel free to call this energy whatever you like, just be aware that there is a sacred energy that flows through you at all times, and the moment you die that energy is redistributed back into the ground from which it came. That energy can be used to commit mass murder or it can be used to heal the world of its problems.

So in summary, Corrupt Power is the power that one uses to manipulate and control the actions, thoughts, ideas, emotions, and opinions of others. It is nasty stuff; however it has served its purpose in assisting humanity to get to where we are today. But we as a species can overcome the desires to manipulate and instead move into total acceptance of others, unconditionally. So the corrupt power is the yang energy, the masculine energy, while the "true power" energy is the yin energy, the feminine, loving, respectful energy. Neither are intrinsically bad. For they both serve a purpose and are allowed to manifest in reality by The Administrators, but we are moving out of the masculine age of conquering via war towards the more subtle age of the feminine spirit.

Don't believe me? Look at the fact that we are more compassionate towards homosexuals than we have been in previous generations. Gays are gaining freedom. Now from a position of judgment, this is a terrible sin, but remember that we are not here to judge. That is not our job as humans and thankfully that is not our responsibility. As far as being homosexual and whether it is a sin or not, I don't think it is any of my business what people choose to do sexually, but I also do not believe it is in humanity's best interest to actively promote it. If gay people want to be gay, let them. Free will is important. But I also think that the respect should be given on both sides. Don't be anti-gay like the God Hates Fags Church, but also don't be teaching that Gay is the new way. Essentially these matters should be addressed openly and logically but not in a way saying that children should become gay, transsexual, and etc.

Transsexuals are especially a sensitive subject, I am aware that some people are born more masculine and more feminine, and various indigenous cultures recognized different sexes than just male and female. They had masculine male, feminine male, and some Native American tribes even acknowledged what was called being "Two Spirit" which was someone who was both a man and a woman inside one sex's body. In summary on the transsexual situation, if someone is transsexual male to female, and they go out with the intention to deceive a man into sleeping with them, they are essentially inviting themselves into a situation that can potentially evoke very strong emotions. This has gotten many transsexual people killed. So either way. We all need to accept responsibility for our actions to complete and total entirety.

Speaking on sin: what is it? For the most part sins are offenses of a tribal cluster. Which is what is one culture's sins are not sins to another and etc. However it is true that there are truly wrong acts people can commit to themselves and others, but generally speaking the sins we have inherited from the previous paradigms are actually just opinions passed down based on tradition of that current understanding.

To expand on that idea: take a look around at the churches in the world that try to vigorously control women. They label them as sluts, heathens, and many other derogatory names for slight infractions such as wearing pants and not obeying their rules. Some of the extremely conservative churches from where I am from prohibit women from wearing make-up, lipstick, pants, and for wanting the right to preach a Sunday service. Are these true sins? Of course not. They are the opinions of a tribal cluster (right or wrong) but they have been taught and passed down to the people through the years, so the people within that circle of understanding have never had the freedom to question the system! So it's okay. I can see why they would teach these ideas though, because it is nice for people to maintain their natural beauty and not obsess over beauty enhancement, but I would not label them sinners for wanting to wear pants. So finally from one perspective one can say that the world is headed exactly to where it is supposed to be, and from another perspective one can say we are depleting our resources and are headed towards destruction.

I say, try not to worry about it too much. Do what you can to contribute to the bettering of the planet and accept responsibility for your actions. Teach this to others and with time corruption will slowly wither away because the people will become more and more aware. Have faith that there is something balancing this Universe and trust that we as humanity can find a balance within ourselves to find a solution to solving the energy and resource problem.

As one last final note for the summary of corrupt power. Corrupt Power is manipulation and deception with the intentional purpose to take away from another in order to benefit oneself. Now that that is wrapped up, let's move on to Understanding Dimension, this is one of my personal favorites. Lets go!

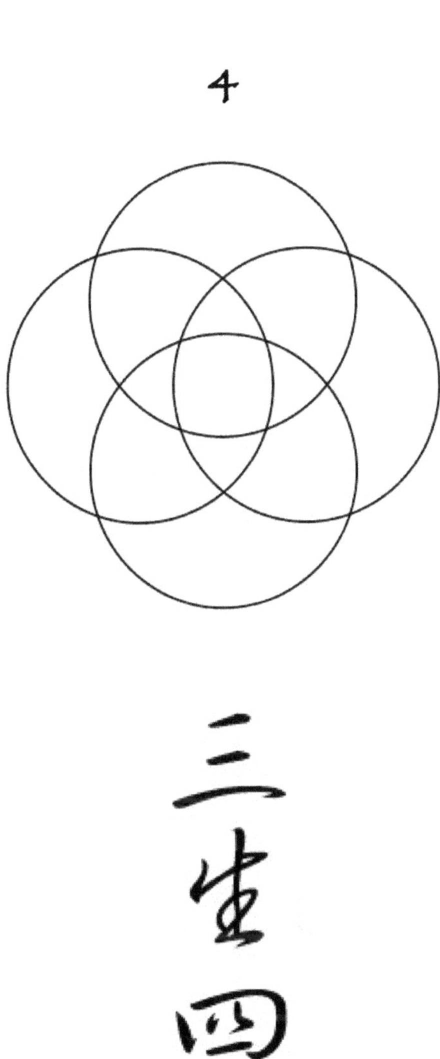

Three creates four

Chapter 4:

Understanding Dimension

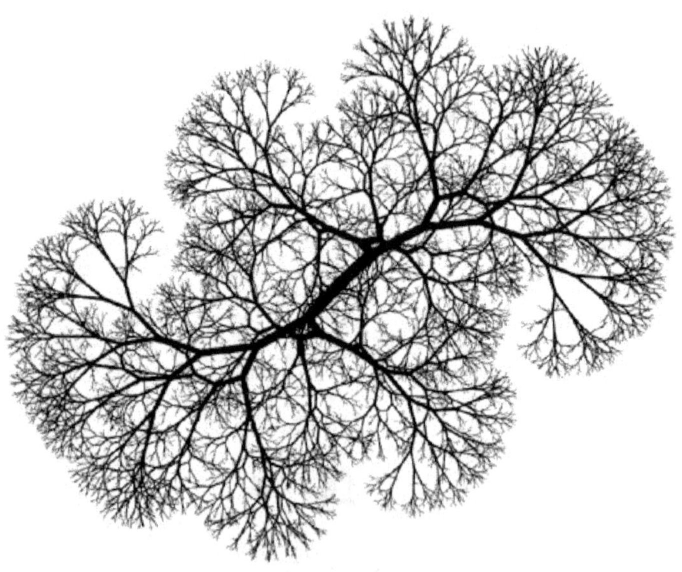

Here's where things begin to get "crazy".

Understanding Dimension

This is a more fun light and hearted chapter, one of my personal favorites. If you have made it this far, I assume I haven't offended or lost you, and if I have offended you, sorry, I didn't mean too; although it will probably only get worse from here on out. In the attempt to expand consciousness things tend to get a little "crazy." And this chapter may certainly expand your mind in some rather bizarre ways, especially if you have no previous understanding of dimension. For those of you that do, this will be a nice rehash and hopefully an interesting different perspective on the curved/closed nature of dimensions.

To start off, you must understand dimensions are curved in on themselves in nature. All dimensions are enclosed, like little bubbles. The metaphysical / physical nature of reality makes this be so, so understand that all dimensions are curved and enclosed in on themselves. Usually there is no way out, unless you can find / create a gap. I'll offer a brief example then cover it in further detail later.

The easiest way to describe a dimension is to think of Earth. Earth is a sphere. You can't leave the Earth unless you escape the coefficient of friction created by gravity and the atmosphere. At around 5 miles per second in a rocket ship you would enter into what is called orbit. You would be forever launched circling the Earth, continuously falling but escaping the earth at the same rate. So in order to escape you would need to travel about 7 miles per second to reach what is called escape velocity. Then you would leave the confines of this Earthly dimension and be permitted to forever drift off into space. So you would Escape one 3D dimensional reality and enter into another. All of these still exist within the same dimension of the 3D physical reality, but this is where Relativity comes into play. This is still relative to the size or dimension of the human being, which is somewhere around 5 to 6 feet tall. So we are still in one dimension even though via the rocket ship we escaped the Circular dimension of the Earth's gravitational field. (It still has a gravitational effect, but not enough to pull you back into that dimensional reality.)

So the physical Earth plane dimension is enclosed, you can't escape unless you create a gap (rocket ship going very fast.) This applies to the spiritual realms also, what is required to blast a ship to outer space? Energy, and lots of it. In this example the energy is a mixture of highly combustible chemicals. Their energy is used to propel the rocket out of the Earth's gravitational influence. So in order to escape the confines of Earth, one has to have a whole lot of energy to expend. Without technology, this would be literally impossible. So now let me offer another example of the enclosed nature of Dimensions.

Anyone with a basic understanding of biology knows what a cell is right? A cell is the basic unit of life. Essentially we are nothing but a compilation of trillions of little tiny living cells, these cells work together on their own, but live independently and create their own energy. So to explain a cell I have attached a photo and try not to get all "egghead" scientific about it. This image should help you see the circular nature of dimensions, in the picture on the next page you will see how the cell is actually like a sphere, not a perfect sphere, but it is basically an enclosed dimension. The Earth is a sphere due to is massive size and therefor its massive gravitational effect. Cells are smaller so they create less gravity, and some cells are even square like.

So if one was a virus, which is much tinier than a cell, it would need to weasel its way inside the cell to begin effecting the specific organelle, but the organelles inside the cell have no way of escaping the confines of the cell unless something rips it out, much like our innards inside our body, our guts. They are staying there unless an outside force pulls them out, so fortunately for us, our guts stay within the dimension of our physical body that exists inside this 3D reality. But all of these examples are still only within the physical dimension. There are supposedly 11 known dimensions aside from these and each dimension is comprised of almost an infinity of dimensions of their own. So understand these examples are dimensions within dimensions.

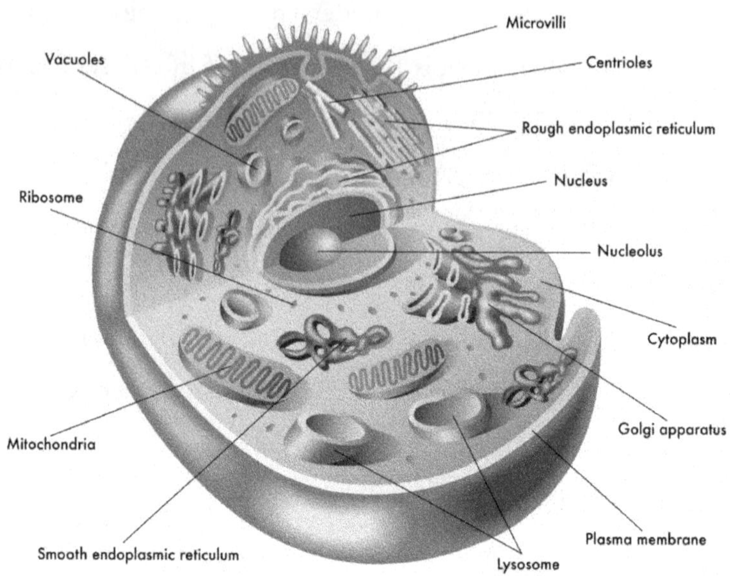

So how does this apply to the book and becoming a Sage? A Sage neglects nothing. Mastery of this understanding begins to magically affect your consciousness to help you manifest change within your world much quicker. In other words, understanding dimension magnifies your hemisphere of influence. For example take medical doctors and the amazingly smart folks who work at the CDC (Center for Disease Control), how are they able to combat viruses and things not visible to the naked eye? By expanding their understanding and increasing their hemisphere of influence. Which is impossible to do without possessing understanding, the more one understands, the larger their hemisphere of influence is and the more potential they have to escape through the various "gaps" of consciousness.

Here is a diagram explaining the expansion of consciousness by the theory of transformational change.

Jean Stead Ph.D *Sustainable Strategic Management: Strategic Management* (2003)

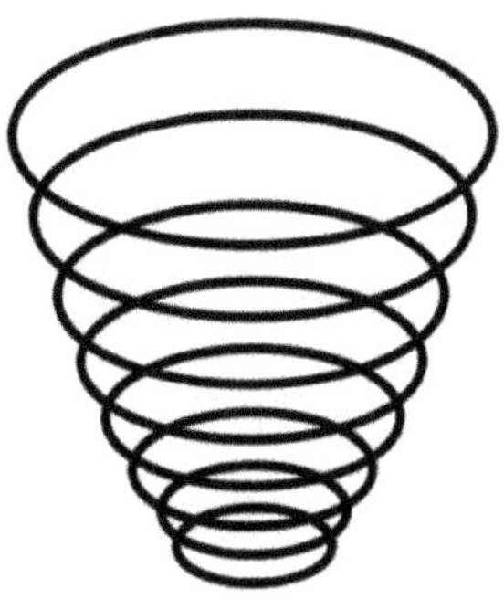

This diagram starts at the bottom and as one's consciousness grows, a better understanding is born, and it continues for as long as there are resources to fuel expansion. As another tie-in to dimension, I am going to show you the most powerful geometric shape that basically is the fractal programming of this natural 3D reality. It is called the Fibonacci Spiral:

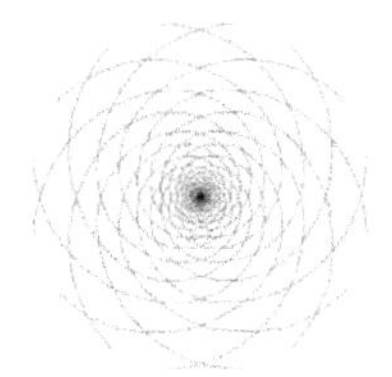

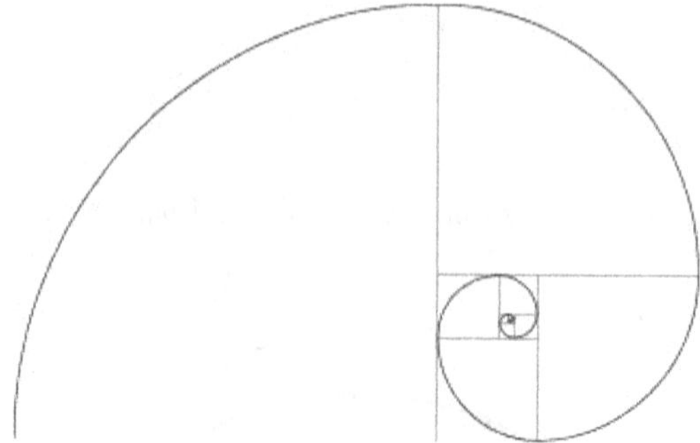

Why is Fibonacci important? Well essentially because it is the mathematical function that all of this 3D matter world adheres to. I will save a more in depth explanation of it for a later book, but instead for brevity I will simply show some images of plants and other "things" that follow this sequence.

As Fibonacci grows from a small rudimentary composition, it uses resources to expand, as it expands from its core it becomes more and more divine, and interestingly enough as it expands further and further, Fibonacci actually approaches the Golden Ratio also known as Phi Φ. So before I lose anyone with unnecessary big and mathematical words, here are the pictures. They better explain it.

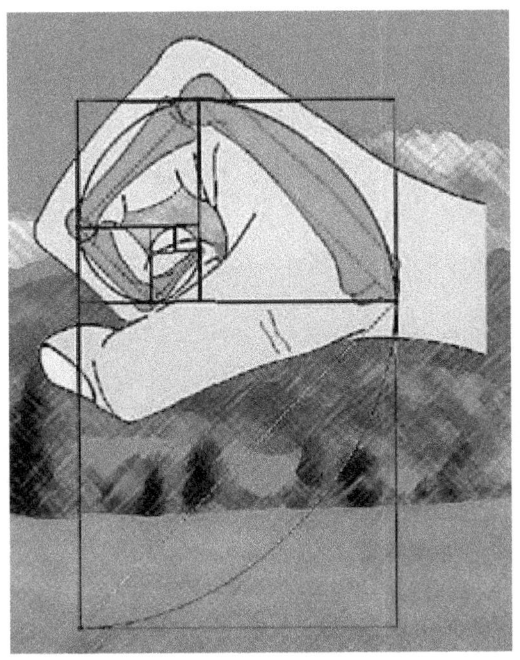

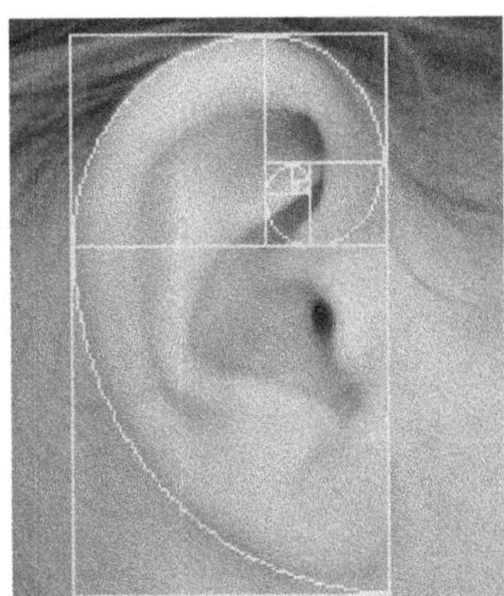

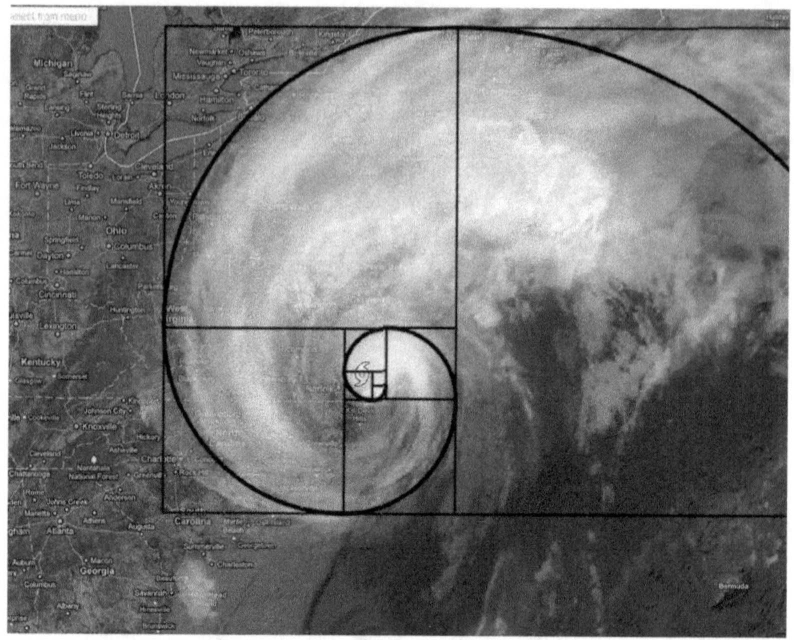

And finally…

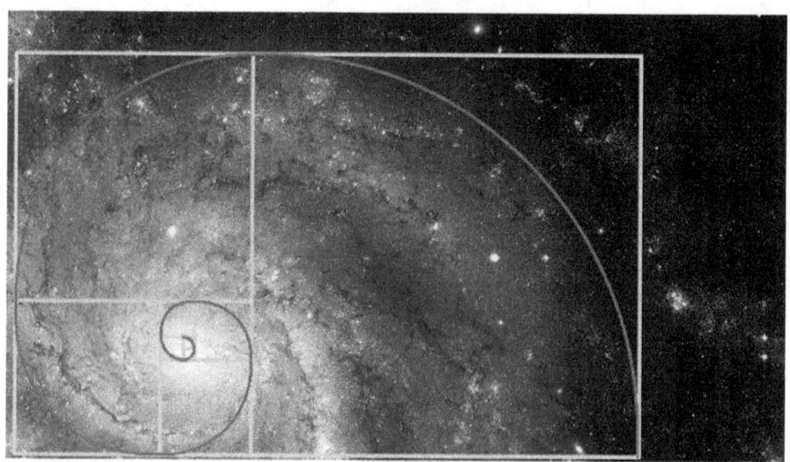

So as you can see, Fibonacci is everywhere. It is one of the fundamental mathematical programs of reality.

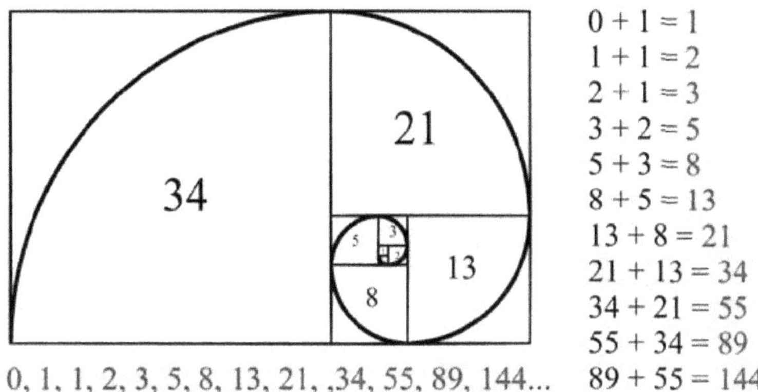

The reason the Fibonacci sequence is so prevalent in nature is because it starts with something very small, crude and rudimentary and over time develops into something more complex - something closer to divinity. Fibonacci begins with 1 a whole number, an integer. It then replicates itself and becomes two, two then becomes three, and it is three that creates all things. This is seen almost literally everywhere in existence. Even in the replication of Embryos. The image on the next page should offer clearer incite on why the Fibonacci Sequence is so important to understand. It is a simple sequence, but the simplest of all is Phi. As Fibonacci expands it approaches the Golden Ratio represented by the Greek Character Phi which is approximately 1.618.

Sacred Geometry & the Creation of a Living Organism

The Stages of Embryo Division

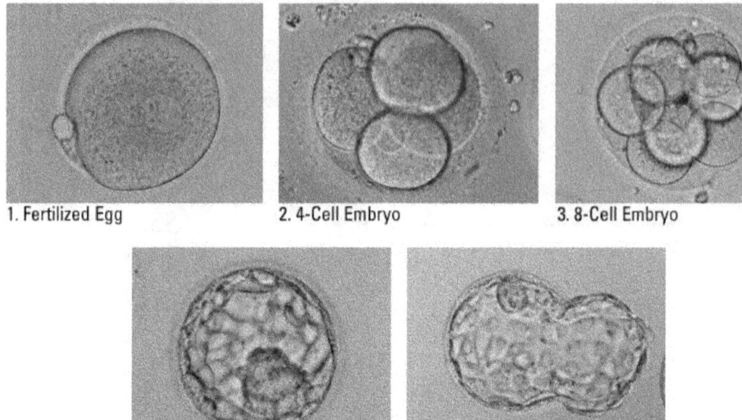

1. Fertilized Egg 2. 4-Cell Embryo 3. 8-Cell Embryo

4. Blastocyst 5. Hatching Blastocyst

With these understandings you can see how literally everything in this 3D world follows very specific and quite simple mathematical functions. The bigger the Universe grows, the more complicated things become. So what is super simple, over time and distance becomes infinitely complicated, but the basic components are all there, just arranged at different levels of complexity.

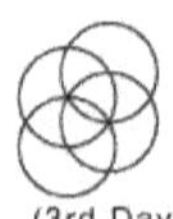

Spherical Octahedron · Vescia Piscis (1st Day) · Tripod of Life (2nd Day) · (3rd Day) · (4th Day) · (5th Day) · (6th Day)

Eventually as God / The Universe / Source/ The Creator / The God-Force or whatever you wish to call it began to come to a certain level of complexity, this created the invention of what we call 3D reality - the 3D matter world - permeating from one dimension into another. The Flower of Life suddenly pops into three dimensions when viewed from a certain perspective. This is how the Universe builds upon itself. It is so simple, but amazingly complex.

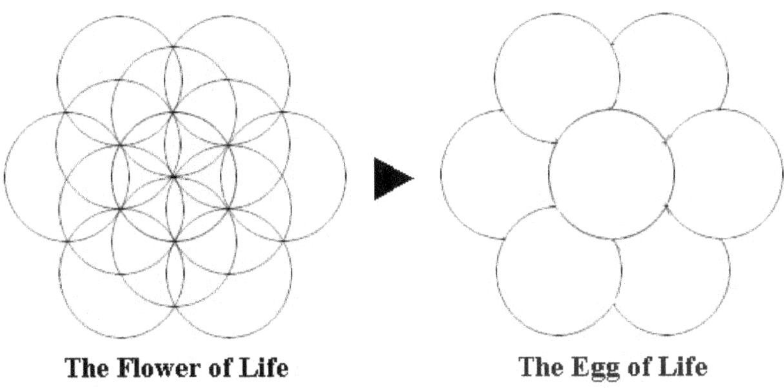

The Flower of Life **The Egg of Life**

These Sacred and very ancient teachings have been censored out of history; they are all there hidden away, but forbidden to be openly spoken about until now. These truths will assist you / humanity to further pull our desires inward and closer to physical reality, as we expand we become more and more "one" with divinity. No matter what it is, the more you something develops it approaches divinity, like a little seed developing into a flower, the power increases. But what Sacred

Geometry teaches is that we are already One with Divinity. The expansion just signifies we are growing more and more complex like creation itself.

This understanding acts as a powerful magnet pulling wisdom to you from other dimensions, the inner-worldly dimensions (thoughts) and beyond, pulling inward to the Physical Dimension (life events / happenings / miracles). So you can think of it as pulling an idea from your creativity and manifesting that idea in the physical world. Like magic your thoughts come from nowhere, electricity of the mind, and manifest magical things into this 3D realm. This is what excites me: creativity. Because with creativity is where the real unlimited potential exists. It is sitting out there someplace in another dimension, and by your force of will, creativity, and concerted action you can manifest it into reality. Now that is magic!

Seriously, look at all of the creative people in movies, TV, Film, authors, and etc. They literally make stuff up and sell it to the people. Finances are an important part of liberation and freedom because money is the energy used to manifest things. So if you increase your understanding of dimension you expand your reality.

So to become financially free you will have to learn to generate what I call Creative Waves. This book was literally a

Creative Wave channeled from the spirit worlds via concerted action and thoughts. What do I mean? I mean I literally have no idea what I am going to type next. I just type and it comes together, piece by piece. But where does it come from? It comes from within my mind. Where does my mind come from? Well to answer this question we need to have the understanding of dimension. How do you get that? By asking questions! Ask the tough questions that makes people cringe, why? Because not knowing evokes an emotional response, they react out of emotion because they simply do not know the answer to the world's biggest questions. So in a way dimension is another one of the forbidden topics. I like those kinds of topics, and I hope you do, or at least you are learning to like them also. It's fun, but it is essential if you want to go anywhere in life. Remember Fibonacci expands closer and closer to divinity. So if you are not expanding in some way, you are wilting and approaching another dimension anyway, death. So expand up and outward, either way when we die, all that we are, is what we made out of our lives and the energy that we contributed to this world.

Moving on to the "Etheric" Dimensions. This is the occult and esoteric stuff that many people refuse to acknowledge, but just because one ignores it, doesn't make it any less real. An ostrich can shove its head in the dirt but that doesn't mean the Lion won't eat it.

In the physical plane we are accustomed to seeking out and obtaining the things that we desire. This is how the normal waking life functions, but in the inner worlds what we call the etheric worlds, everything acts in reverse. Let me explain what the etheric worlds are. There are many layers of reality that exist simultaneously. There are worlds within worlds folded up on top of each other, some are interconnected and others are not, but they all exist right here, right now, some even before our very eyes, and others just at the reach of the back of our eyelids.

There are several ways to perceive these worlds, but as you probably can assume it requires a "powerful" imagination. Your mind can conjure up all sorts of things and thankfully the moment you imagine something it doesn't automatically appear. Your mind learned to shut that off long ago. I can distinctly remember the day when I was about 13 years old, I was laying on the floor playing with army men. I was trying to imagine a river that he was going across the carpet, when suddenly: some type of hormone or something was released in my brain and I thought "what the heck am I doing?" And just like that, my child-like imagination was shutoff. It shut off due to the nature of Fibonacci, I was now going through puberty and that meant I needed to become prepared to reproduce at age 13 and a child-like imagination wasn't very cool with the popular girls… It actually was, they were just too stupid to see it. I know all. Ha

But now, today I am working on rekindling that child-like magical mind power — to reawaken my childlike imagination and perceive the worlds that were revealed to me as a child. (P.S. It's back)

As a child I could instantly imagine a 100 foot monster it would magically appear. I can remember being two years old talking to my commander, his name was Spike. Spike gave me missions around the yard, I would go and throw walnuts at trees, and other heroic adventures, but now, that heroic mission has changed. It is still there, but now it's a little more difficult for me to hear Spike radioing into my ear what I need to do next.

I assume it might be that way for other people also and maybe some adults can still visualize a 100 foot monster in front of them, not sure why anyone would want too, but thankfully the way the Etheric dimensions work there is a time delay on how quick things can manifest, and there are certain limits in this physical reality as to what can enter this dimension. Think about this: how long did it take for the idea of an automobile to manifest? I mean people were riddin' around in buggies for thousands of years, but one faithful day, BAM! We got the car.

So how does one perceive these other realms where unlimited creativity, inspiration, and ideas are stored? One way to perceive these other worlds is by entering into trance and through deep relaxation and meditation. This is the best way because it requires discipline and pure focus.

Exercise and discipline both help, because your body is a closed or open system, depending on how you look at it. So the food you eat and the condition of your heart and other organs are important. But as basic as it goes, your brain is the most important. So you need a healthy brain in order to reach your fullest potential.

The fastest and most profound way to begin expanding one's creativity and to acquire the perception of these, "other worldly experiences" is to quite simply, straight out… "Wait! And be patient!" LS Deangelo spoke up. He said: "Isn't it interesting how these so called 'entheogenic' plants have been seen around the world for thousands of year, yet no one, not even a single soul understands their point or purpose?

Me, well... I thought. I thought I knew, but I wasn't tellin'. Perhaps, I might have jumped right into the energy of that Morning, boy wasn't it a Glory, the sun was shining and everything was in perfect harmony. "What beautiful seeds." Said Mr. Deangelo, but he pointed out that meditation is the true key.

Meditation as defined by Chung Fu in the book *Under the Plum Tree,* is nothing more than deep relaxation. But I honestly don't believe you can get there without stepping through the

Matrix by the use of the beans Jack had, he did climb the beanstalk. "Had to be magic." One could write an entire book on the positive spiritual impact of such things, but would be prohibited from speaking about it out of ridicule, fear, failure, and worst of all! Poison! Socrates, he got the poison. At least he was 70 though. So for simplicity, I will just say this: they grow abundantly all over the world, they are well documented for their benefits and the deep intimate spiritual relationship not only with mankind, but also countless other species that live here on Earth. Take the reindeer for example, they love the mushroom. Ever wondered where the idea of Santa Clause came from? Well I will tell you, Santa was a Siberian shaman that gave mushrooms to people as gifts, he was a saint, a healer, a medicine man, he was a spiritual teacher. Due to some editing of history that I won't get into here, basically our shamanic past has been taken away from us over greed and corruption and for profit of controlling people. This may seem like a harsh statement, but it is obvious once you understand the nature of humans and the relationships of spiritual plants. I will try to explain this the clearest way I can for someone who has literally no idea of entheogenic plants. Entheogen means God within, so these plants help one reconnect with nature, with spirit, with the divine creator. I think I have pretty good evidence that will be hard to deny and it will help you see the relevance to modern culture.

Some of these ideas came from James Authors Book *Mushrooms and Mankind,* but it is basically my own research and original thoughts. His book is worth reading, but I don't agree with everything he wrote.

Did you know that Amanita Muscaria (the Mario mushroom) is a powerful consciousness altering mushroom that has been used for spiritual practices for thousands of years? It grows abundantly all over the world. And the most profound discovery that I made is the mushroom also grows in a symbiotic relationship with Christmas trees; meaning that the mushroom and Christmas tree live together in perfect harmony. They literally only grow where coniferous trees are because somehow they grow off the roots. But they are especially found growing under Christmas trees. Ever wondered why Christmas colors are red, white, and green? Ever wondered why there are presents wrapped in red and white under Christmas trees? Ever wondered why we have stockings hanging on the fire place mantle? Ever wondered why the hell Reindeer can fly??? Not to mention how can Santa be everywhere at once? Seriously, deliver presents to every child around the world all in one night. Well I will tell ya, it's a metaphor.

So here we go. I must warn you though, once you read this you can't unlearn it, you will never view the Christmas holiday the same again, and it may even make you question other things about this world that you may have never previously questioned. So if you want to back away and not learn the truth behind the Christmas traditions and the relationship to Shamanism, here is your last chance.... Good, Neo, let's get out of here. In recent centuries of the past, our ancestors in various parts of the world, most notably in Europe where many of the modern Christian holiday traditions originated, the peoples that were there were what is now classified as "Pagan" which holds a negative connotation, but it simply means "natural Earth religion." Specifically referring to the Christmas & Santa tale, the medicine men (shamans) would gather the Amanita mushrooms (common name Fly Agaric) from under the Christmas trees, and to prevent the Sacred Mushrooms from rotting they were placed in socks and hung above the mantle on the fire place. This process dried the mushrooms out to ensure they would be available for later use, for later spiritual ceremonies. The entire holiday of Christmas is an intimate story of Shamanism and the blessing of the mushroom provided by Earth. Magic mushrooms are also called Earth's tongue, because this is how nature can directly communicate to people and other organisms.

It makes sense from a logical point of view though, Mother Earth provides, food and water for our bodies, and other Sacred plants for our spirit. It is the truth, I promise, I wouldn't lie or make this stuff up, this is well known history. If you are Christian it may challenge your beliefs, but you must realize the Catholic Church / Roman Empire had an agenda when they were conquering the "Pagan" peoples. Christianity was deemed the official religion of Rome and when they began integrating Christianity into the "pagan" people's way of life, they allowed them to keep some of their traditions, many of which have survived until today. Christmas is one of them. If you would like a more indepth analysis of this subject go to google and type in "The truth about magic mushrooms", my website, TheTruthAwaits.com should popup pretty close to the top. There are pictures and videos and such there. Moving on.

We as a modern society are so far removed from our connection to Earth it is sad, we need to expand our consciousness and reconnect with the Earth's spirit if we wish to survive as a species, the Earth will be fine, but it is us and our way of life that is at risk.

But Mother Earth, she is alive. You don't think we are the only living things do you? I mean Mother Earth even made us. Even the Bible say: "we were made from the dust of the Earth." We came from the Earth, the Earth is a living organism that grows and evolves, it is not just a hunk of rock floating around in space. Nope, she is our mother and we should respect her. Before I get too carried away speaking about the importance of entheogenic plants and expanding consciousness, let's move back to the other dimensions I speak of. But one last final note before we move on. This is a good one:

Okay, if you and I are conscious of ourselves, and we both agree that we were made from the dust of the Earth, and the Earth came from the Universe, then what does that mean?

It means a part of the Universe is conscious of itself. Therefore the Universe is consciousness. A part of the Universe is conscious of itself, therefor, the UNIVERSE is CONSCIOUS! All of it is alive, some to varying degrees to another, but everything exudes the God-Force. A rock, a pillow, a mushroom, a dung beetle, a dog, stars, and of course us meager little humans. To me, this is my perspective of God. The Alpha, the Omega, the beginning, and the end; If the Universe is infinite and God is infinite, then the Universe IS a manifestation of God.

Okay getting back to Understanding Dimension. This is a broad topic and probably deserves a book or 20 of its own. I am going to try and further explain other dimensions scientifically. As I said, there are dimensions all over the place, if you are interested in physics you will know that the universe behaves considerably differently depending on your relative position. Recapping on an earlier statement in this chapter, the simplest way to describe this idea is to have you imagine you are inside an animal cell. Scientists define a cell as the most basic unit of life. Within a cell is an entire world of things that only exist inside the cellular dimension. They exist in both worlds, but relative to the position, Mitochondria could never exist outside of a cell, at least not naturally. Mitochondria only exist within the dimensions of a cell. Mitochondria are organelles that help with metabolism and the survival of the cell. You can think of it as a cellular power plant. All cells are compiled to create an organ or tissue. A heart consists of billions of interconnected heart cells that function in unison to make a living heart. A liver consists of billions of liver cells, and so on and so forth. Inside of the cell contains the entire dimension reality of that cell. For example: a pizza does not exist in the cellular world, but mitochondria could exist inside a pizza (assuming it has toppings with eukaryotic cells). The laws of physics have a tendency to bend and change the bigger or smaller you travel. Inside of a cell everything is suspended in a gel like substance called cytoplasm so within the dimension of a cell everything kind of floats around or is supported by the cytoskeleton, and things inside are affected differently than we are here right now. These are two realities that exist simultaneously, but they are happening at the same time and even within the same body. Interesting is it not?

The cellular dimension is just one small example of the possibly millions of dimensions that could exist. The reason I classify them as alternate dimensions is because different variables exist within the differing natural worlds, and most importantly the laws of nature drastically change. A general rule of thumb is the smaller you go, the more the physics and natural laws change. This is a major issue with subatomic physics and cosmology. Scientists are vigorously trying to create a theory that mathematically combines the two together, but this seems to be exceedingly difficult because we really have no way of observing at the subatomic level, yet. Stephen Hawking was able to tie together Einstein's theories of Relativity, but still we are seeking a total understanding of the physical world. My purpose is to integrate the spiritual with the physical, this is called metaphysics.

A good example of the laws bending at the subatomic dimension is with the omission of the law of gravity. Normally we experience gravity 24 hours a day seven days a week, but if you were to travel inside an atom, say someplace inside an animal cell, the laws of gravity no longer apply, at least to our current understanding. This is why physicists have difficulty combining the astronomical with the subatomic. To explain it a little more clearly it is a living paradox. Everything on Earth experiences the force of gravity, but the particles Earth is composed of are omitted from the forces of gravity. This is one reason physicist have postulated the idea of a gravitron: a particle of gravity that attracts matter. The idea of a gravitron works because it explains why at the subatomic level gravity doesn't exist. The reason being, gravity affects the dimension outside, not the dimension inside.

A rather crude way you could think of this is to imagine attaching a rope to a house that is built on top of a cart, and pulling said cart with a Mac Truck, the rope is not directly pulling you, but it is pulling the thing you are sitting inside of. So you are free to move about inside, do jumping jacks, poor a glass of milk, play fetch, and basically anything else you could do outside. Relative to your position you are unaffected; but if you were to stick your head out the window and leave the confines of your inner home dimension, you would realize your brother who is driving the 18 wheeler has you whizzing down the highway at 90 miles per hour headed straight towards the drive through of Mc Donald's.

So far the trend is the deeper and smaller you travel, the increasingly different the worlds become. Inside of an atom it is mostly empty space, with the exception of some charged particles chaotically buzzing around. Physicists know much of this to be fact because of different observations and studies they have done. If you have a hard time believing in something you can't see, and we really have no way to see them directly, let me offer another thought. Many years ago in the early 1900's scientists were beginning the early studies of radiation. The theory existed that atoms could be split and create vast amounts of energy, enough to power the worlds energy a million times over. Time went on and Einstein's theory was proved to be true, but that same power that can be used to energize the Earth can also be used to destroy the Earth, and so the Atom Bomb was created. It was all based on theory, but later proven to be true, for better or for worse. $E=MC^2$ or Energy is equal to the mass of the said object times the square of the electricity it possesses. C is the variable for the speed of light. I am not a physicist so I can't go into much detail, but I do know enough to see this is true. Think of this, this is not directly the same but it can explain it in a crude way. When you are cold you throw some logs into the fire and the logs are converted into radiation energy. So the $E=MC^2$ equation is explaining physical matter contains energy that can be radiated outwards to release extreme amounts of energy. Building a fire is not near as efficient as splitting atoms, but it helps get the point across. If I remember from my physics class correctly a single penny contains enough energy to power a single 100 watt light bulb for something like 60 years. The problem is preventing the energy from releasing elsewhere.

Not a whole lot was known about the universe much smaller than the elemental level, which is the boarder of physical reality. There were many ideas way early on you have probably heard of, a thoroughly common one is the Classical Element theory that has been believed by various ancient cultures. They believed everything in the universe consisted of combinations of Earth, Fire, Water, and Air. Some instances there were an additional element of Spirit and some modes of thought believed in something called the Ether. That was the most popular mental construct for millennia throughout the world until modern science. Chemistry and Science wasn't formally created until 1789. And through the Scientific Method we have advanced to where we are today.

So now we have talked about the very small dimensions, but now let's talk about what happens if we zoom out. Again gravity is another point of interest because it is the most fundamental force. We experience gravity here on Earth, gravity is what keeps everything in place, but let's imagine we are the size of Earth. What is gravity doing now? It is pulling in on itself. So it is no longer a downward force, but it is now a compressive force much like what we would experience if we were 6 miles under the ocean, this is the experience of Gravity in conjunction of mass. Weight is a variable that is dependent on gravity. This is what creates the circular effect of objects in space, gravity. Everything compresses in on itself, and you could only imagine what it would be like if an object were the size of the Milky Way Galaxy, the galaxies are affected by gravity, but now it's a tugging and pulling between each other type of force. So you get the point. There is probably an unlimited number of dimensions out there. There would almost have to be especially when you are dealing with numbers approaching infinity. I believe the universe is infinite and therefor there is no end from the positive infinity to the negative infinity. Or as a lady said in a popular Physics seminar, "its turtles all the way down." This was in reference of the popularly believed myths that land came out of the sea as a turtles back. It is similar to which came first? The chicken or the egg? We live in a fractal programmed world. Things come out of each other like those little Russian Dolls. There is always another doll. The best evidence for the fractal programming of the world is the fact people come out of other people. If you look at a tree the programming of the tree makes it be what it is, directed by sunlight the tree grows up, closer to warmth.

For some time we have only been talking about the physical dimensions, but that is only the beginning. The physical dimensions were necessary to begin explaining the concepts here to follow. Now I want you to become familiar with the dimensions available inside of your own head, the dimension of the human mind.

The internal worlds are the dimensions I have really become fascinated with. It is this dimension that the world's great thinks have drawn their inspiration from, ancient monks would meditate on the infinity within their minds, partially due to a lack of external engagement in a less technically complicated world, and I also believe it was due to a deeper connection to the spiritual world. They were deeper connected to nature. They are right here, right, now, and available to anyone to experience with patience, practice, and time. So how do we begin? I guess I will begin with the current dimension you are probably experiencing right now as you read. This dimension is called waking reality. It is the state everyone is familiar with and is the normal waking reality that we go about during our day. The purpose of this state is to ensure the survival of our physical bodies that we are attached to. Here you go about your daily life, washing the dog, eating pizza, going to school, and so on. The interesting thing is waking reality consists of many different layers that are on top of each other directly vertical, kind of like a sandwich on a table. The layers have five broad categories starting from the fastest to slowest. Gamma, Beta, Alpha, Theta, and Delta there may be more but anything below Delta means you're practically dead because all brain activity has stopped. Anything above Gamma would be totally chaotic and I'd assume you might go crazy. The brain has these balanced pretty well.

Right now depending on your level of excitement and focus you are probably in Beta state which exists at around a brainwave speed of 14-30 Hz. This is where the majority of the world lives day to day. This is the daily working state at which most of us experience daily reality. Directly above that is Gamma, which is like a hyper focused reality where hyper analytical and so the called super learning takes place. This can be thought of as Einstein brain. If you were taking a calculus exam it would be helpful to achieve this state. It lies around 30-100 Hz. I associate this brain state with "smart drugs" such as stimulants. I don't believe scientists have officially announced this as fact yet, but this is something I have personally discovered and evidence holds it to be true.

Below both of those is Alpha. Alpha is where relaxation and light meditation occurs. This will probably be the first parallel reality you will experience. It is categorized around 9-13 Hz, time slows and your perception of reality begins to shift, your internal dialogue begins to change as the Ego drifts off to quietness and your Higher Self is awakened. You can think of yourself being a sandwich of two different people, your personality and your Spirit. Your personality is your Ego; it is selfish and wants to protect itself. Its purpose is to make the physical body do all sorts of things in order to continue to survive. The Spirit you also known as the Higher Self it is the true you. It is the real you. The caring, loving, and eternal you that knows best and gently guides you while your ego just tries to survive. It is the Higher Self. Many cultures have mistaken your intuition/Higher Self as an external force because the Ego is unfamiliar with it, but your Spirit Guide is just another term for your Higher Self. They are one in the same clouded by the arrogance and ignorance of the Ego. In most people the Ego reigns supreme because the ego deals with necessary things such as survival, but once you quite the Ego you will be introduced to the real you. Perhaps you already have, anyway we are a sandwich of beings living within the sandwich of reality. I like the sounds of that.

If you slow your brain down even slower and your Higher Self travels deeper into the dimension of your mind you will enter the dimension of the Theta state which exists around 4-8 Hz. At this state the body is usually in a deep sleep and your conscious mind is separated from the body. Meaning you can't feel your fingers, arms, or anything else for that matter. You are simply a consciousness floating around inside your and you will only visualize what your mind's eye is capable of perceiving. Here your eyes are starting to shut off; you may experience some flashes and wisps of light that is just the electricity of the mind. Theta is where many of the inner worlds begin to reveal themselves because now the body is asleep and the Ego is battled into submission. It leaves the Higher Self total freedom to explore. The deeper into trance you go the more there is to discover. Theta is the trance state of Zen Masters there has been thousands of years of practice and research spent on the Theta state, and it isn't very difficult to reach. You just have to stay perfectly still until your body is disassociated from the mind.

It sounds scary, but once you are there it is very enlightening and inspiring. This is also where deep sleep and trance occurs. There is one more state known called Delta. It is the lowest state where not a whole lot of information is known. Delta is the comatose state. It's very slow and usually nothing is experienced that can be remembered anyway. When someone has a car wreck and is put in a coma for 6 months they are probably in Delta state. This is the reason they don't remember anything when they awake. The mind is slowed so slow in an attempt to keep the physical body alive nothing is remembered.

So now you know when I talk about different worlds realize what I really mean is just a different perception of this world based on the vibrational frequency of the brain. I associate the upwards and downwards explanation because in trance this is the sensation that I feel. The height is correlated with the speed. They all are truly the same reality, but they are perceived from different states of consciousness. They all exist simultaneously but can only be perceived or experienced at various states of brain speed and function, you can literally go out of body and travel through the worlds, but the first step is becoming aware of what is going on here right now, right around you. Then you can move on to trying to perceive the Etheric forces and inner worldly dimensions. I am by no means a master at this stuff either. If anything I am just getting started, one of my teachers, Chime 1.3.0 said that many people get beginners syndrome and after a few years of practice, they think they know it all. Well I learned he was referring to me. He is an interesting dude. Check out his book if you want to learn more about him, it is called The Children of R. It is out there, I mean way out there, like deep space out there, but his perspective on things is interesting.

Now that this chapter is wrapped up and you have an Understanding of Dimension, let us move on to chapter 5, the secret of Internalizing your Thoughts. This is a powerful step to take in perceiving the bizarre and strange worlds around us.

Chapter 5:

Internalize Your Thoughts

Internalize Your Thoughts

As I mentioned in an earlier chapter true power is an internal manifestation of Will Power and self-control. The first step in creating internal power is you must begin to control your speech and dialogue both with others and how you communicate with yourself. This is a powerful discipline because when the chatter of the mind goes quiet is when real wisdom is able to be perceived. It is essentially shutting out all distractions and falling out of this world and into another one.

To begin with begin to internalize your accomplishments, goals, plans, and so on. If you plan to quit smoking cigarettes don't tell a single soul, because when you speak it, you disempower yourself. There is strength in silence; I will talk about this more in a later chapter. Silence and internalizing / consolidating your energy is perhaps the most important step in obtaining higher consciousness because your reality flows from what you think and say. For example: you say "man I am having a bad day." This is an affirmation that your day is bad which is speaking a personal opinion into a factual truth. When it's not, it's an opinion. All conflict is simply a divergence of opinions. So if you must speak anything to anyone, make sure it is a positive affirmation, unless the negative is the truth, for example:

You can't say your dog was run over by a train, but he is okay. Just try and be as positive as possible when dealing with life, joke, have fun, and keep your opinions to yourself, unless you're a writer then you can write whatever the hell you want, just be aware no matter what, you can't please everybody and doing so will be at a compromise of your intention…

So why bother with all of this internalizing your true self talk? Because the ego personality creates an ideal model of how things should be and when something is outside of what the ego wants, conflict is created. So the events that cause a bad day to one person may be gentle effort to another. So instead of confirming it as a reality, just accept what you are experiencing and take note of it. Select your words wisely. All anguish can generally be redirected and communication usually helps. If you internalize your "Emotional responses" to other people's actions, you limit the power that they can have over you.

There are some pretty wicked people in this world, I know I have said before that Evil didn't exist, well I was wrong. It does, and some people delight in controlling others. So the less you give people the less they can hold over you. Now this doesn't mean to walk around like a robot. No way. Just be mindful of what you do share. And be mindful of how you respond to external stimuli.

Here is another example that will add further clarity with responding to external stimuli; the next time you stub your toe while wandering around carelessly in the dark, instead of releasing a negative "curse" release that with a joyful laugh. It is funny anyway. Why would you do that to yourself? Chances are you deserve the stubbed toe for being reckless. Laugh it off and next time turn on the lights. All physical pain is subject to opinion anyway. Remember that.

Moving on, we are a spiritual body inside a physical body. All of your physical power exists in 3D reality, but the real you. Your Higher Self is an infinite energy that literally has always existed and will always exist. One way to understand this concept is "you are what you eat." Now you may ask me "what in the world does this mean?" Okay. So you eat a hotdog. The hotdog is digested in your stomach the calories of the hotdog go towards your metabolism and what isn't used is stored as fat. Okay so where does the hotdog come from? Assuming it is a beef hotdog it comes from a cow. The cow's energy is redistributed through your body and it makes you grow and thrive. The cow got its energy from the grass. The grass received its energy from photosynthesis which is from solar energy, light.

The Sun provides energy for all plants, but where does the sun get energy from?

The sun creates radiation/heat/light energy through the nuclear process of fusion, which is fusing very light elements such as hydrogen into heavier elements such as helium. Now where did the energy inside the Hydrogen come from? (This is the revelation of the equation of $E=MC^2$ which was Einstein's correlation between Energy and Mass.) Scientists basically say energy has existed forever because we have observed it cannot be created nor destroyed, just rearranged. So you, me, the dog, the cat, the refrigerator, your uncles beard, the sofa, are all the same, but they are just different reincarnations of the same basic substance. A higher evolution if you will. This substance is unknown; scientists have narrowed it down past the atom so small to where they are creating different theories to explain the universe. String Theory is a popular one, but it is my personal opinion it is not complete because it goes on forever. It is a fractal that continuously gets smaller and smaller. Everything is made of something and it goes from the positive infinity to the negative infinity, infinitely big and infinitely small. This leads us to what many refer to as the God Force, God, the Universal Law, The Dao, The Tao, and many other titles to explain the Universe.

So we have all existed forever and ever in some form just not in this physical body. We are a part of the God-Force. We are an essential piece of the Universe. It is only by habit we view ourselves separate from God. We are a part of God and God is a part of us. With this knowledge comes great power and humility. When you consciously realize you are a part God it is very humbling. Suddenly many of the frustrations of life fade away and eventually we can enter the great quite of the Universal mind.

Now do you see we are infinite and internal beings? We have always existed and always will exist. Most problems are very small and only relevant to the ego. It is only our ego personality that is external from the rest of the world. The ego is like a spoiled child always demanding more. It wants to be treated special; it wants observers, admirers, and all of that unnecessary clutter. The infinite you, the Higher You does not need any of that. The reason the ego wants to be special is because by being special you feel safer, higher than others, and somehow closer to God. By being closer to God the ego thinks it will live longer. The ego's only purpose is to ensure your physical survival. But it needs to be disciplined and controlled to allow you to reach your fullest potential. In reality as I said you already are close to God. No one is any closer than the other, it is only by personal opinion that you are or are not. We are all already as close as we can get to the God-Force because we are a part of the God-Force. We are a piece of the Universe. Here is something to fuel your mind. So if we are a part of the Universe and we are conscious of ourselves and of others, that means a part of the Universe is alive and conscious of itself. This is what postulates the idea the Universe in fact is God.

Now if you think God is external and somehow not a part of the Universe this is probably due to your cultural upbringing. Many cultures externalize God, while others are known for accepting we are all a part of the system. I believe the externalization of a humanoid God is the reason so many people refuse to believe in a God. Religions pass on great stories about a man who was on Earth that was so great that he had to be God. This is hard to believe and many reject it. Then you have more complications of the trinity, and etc. Which confuse people even more. The Muslims say Mohammad is the divine one connected to God and the Christians argue that no it was not Mohammad, but Jesus. They are all equally true in some ways and equally wrong in others, since we are a part of creation, all of us is a small tinsy-tiny part of God.

However, what most religions teach is often geared for their benefit; it is what is best for their society and their congregation, not the whole. Almost all religions are forms of entrapment in one way or another. They seek to draw you in and make you loyal to their system and their way of life. They do this because everyone wants everyone else to support them and their beliefs. Many can't question it so they have no other choice but to support it and find reasons to support their beliefs, their rules, regulations, and etc.

If you contradict what they teach you are then labeled an infidel, secular, or Pagan. If you see the similarities in the past three terms it's because they are all the same concepts. It basically says "Anyone who doesn't believe like me is going to Hell and is dangerous to my way of life." So they are banished, burned at the stake, and eliminated so they are no longer a threat to their collective ego. It's quite silly and tribal really.

What we seek to do is become un-entrapped and free. This is the path to enlightenment it's not how much money you donate to the ashram. It's about growing and maturing spiritually that matters. It's about being free and not infringing on other people. It's about escaping the egos needs to control others, and focusing on what others really need.

Be strong and stand straight in life. Do not lean and infringe on other people. Weak people are constantly begging for attention and demanding to be noticed. Don't try and be cool, don't try and be any certain way, and most importantly don't try and be something that you are not. Just be you to the best of your abilities. Work hard and make progress, but stop caring if anyone notices. Besides a Sage does not care what others think of them. A Sage should also have no opinions of how other people should be. If someone is a certain way and it bugs you, that's okay. But don't judge them for it because we don't know the whole picture. You can help them if they ask for help, but in general don't help if they don't ask for it. How often has someone tried to give you advice and their advice unwanted? It is annoying to be begin with and most of the time people will only help themselves when they are good in ready to be helped. So what if it takes 50 years for someone to change. We are eternal and therefore we can wait a lifetime if we have too.

Be patient and visualize what you want. Think on it. See it manifesting before your eyes. When the time is right the Universe will provide the appropriate path for you, and if not, so what? Maybe that new car would have been too much for you to handle and having it would have made you a slave to the payments. There is always another option, just be flexible and try and never be ridged, ridged things break.

Now this is not to say you shouldn't get what you want. It is perfectly okay to get what you want, but there must be concerted action in obtaining your goals. The trick is to not run all over town wasting energy desperately trying to find the solution, if it turns up, then great. If it doesn't then you don't need it anyway. Think of it like a car salesman. The more you show the salesman that you want the car the more he will be willing to charge you for it. Stuart Wilde called it "Wanting it Tax in his book *Silent Power.* The more you want something the more you are willing to pay for it. Now to reframe your mind; the way to pay almost nothing is to not want it in the first place! "If you don't want it you don't need it, and if you do get it, it will be by your means only."

Let me give you an example: one day while I was running a storefront, a very wiry and energetic man came in offering to sell us a cleaning product. He was very talkative and much fun to watch, definitely a natural salesman. He immediately began searching about and located a stain on the carpet. Without missing a beat he started spraying the mystery liquid all over the floor. With one violent swap of the food stain was magically gone. The cleaner worked great, the stain he removed had been there for years. He then went on with his sales pitch; he told us this amazing cleaner could be ours for one easy payment of $79.95. Preposterous! No cleaner is worth $80 a bottle! We liked the product and the demonstration, but we didn't like it that much. So to prove how great the cleaner is he proceeded to clean another spot, and another, and another, until he almost cleaned most of the stains off the carpet. Eventually he realized we were not going to chunk over any money and left. He already done the work, but we were not going to stop him. About five minutes later, he came right back in and said "listen just for you I will give it to you today for only $10! He dropped his price a whopping 88%!

Just to have him leave we bought the product. The cleaner turned out to be a scam and does not remove stains other than dirt. But a lesson was learned. Just think of how many people are tricked by the sales pitch or pay the full $80 to make him leave. You can almost always get a better deal; you just have to wait it out. Some people feel pressured to buy, but basically he was infringing on our time and privacy by being inconsiderate of our time, he didn't ask if we wanted to see his demonstration he just jumped in. He was relying on us to give in, and give him what he wants. He simply wanted to win. When you think about it, winning is nothing more than outlasting your opponent. Whoever who has the most will power wins.

More often than not whoever loses, usually gives up, whether they consciously realize it or not. Sure skill is involved in sports and other physical activities, but a team who really wants to win will overcome the obstacles. It is will power that matters the most, not to mention Will Power is exercised, the brain can be exercised to endure, so that in conjunction with physical training betters your chances for success.

Hopefully you will find this book to be a quick and delightful read. It takes a certain level of Will Power to read a book. I know I was certainly not a heavy reader when I was younger. Now I believe reading is a great discipline that helps build will power and it also benefits you with stories and experiences.

It is all on you. It is your responsibility and no one else's. Concentration is needed, for without concentration your power is weak and diffused. Your power lies in where your concentration flows. It is interesting how the mind plays tricks on you. You will be reading a page and your ego will be fidgeting trying to make you move, scratch, want a cup of coffee, but if you can just endure for a few minutes the ego learns to be quite. It goes to sleep, until you decide to give it control again.

Enlightenment has been described as putting the ego in an extended sleep, to allow peacefulness and a removal of the desires and whims of the mind. As I've said True Power is not given; it is cultivated with Will Power and concentration, in order to move forward the ego must be conquered. It needs to learn you are in charge now. If not then it can ruin your life, I am sure most people have been lead down a stray path that was pleasing to the ego. And eventually they realized they were better off from where they came. The ego is funny in that way. Somehow it finds a way of finding faults in perfectly fine situations. Say you are dating a beautiful lady for months attempting to win her affection, finally she succumbs to your advances and now you have her. You enter into an exclusive relationship and a few months later you find yourself desiring a change of scenery. You think of how green the grass is on the other side. Sometimes this is true and sometimes it is not. This is because there is no perfect man or woman. There is no perfect situation. All situations are perfectly imperfect. Or you could even say all things are perfect it is only the ego's opinion that it is imperfect.

The lesson here is to find perfection in every situation. If both people believed the relationship was perfect then it in fact is perfect and without flaws, but the trick is the timing to be right and you both believe the same thing simultaneously. The goal is to fervently believe in the mutual love and actively resist the desires for change. Now you can see the importance of disciplining the ego and no allowing it to drive your life.

Humans are weak and frail little creatures, we are nothing more than a sack of walking meat, some of us may be strong and think that we are tough, but in the end we are just small little life forms trying to survive. Be strong, think strong, and live strong. Be happy with what you have. Perhaps your situation is unhealthy or truly bad for you and your partner, then fine, change it, but remember you must be happy with what you have right now if you ever plan on finding lasting happiness. Accept what you have, but make no commitment if you are not 100% certain this is where you need to be. Internalize your unhappiness because speaking it just reassures it into existence.

What do you think is a powerful person would do? Would they squack around complaining that their life is a mess? No, they would internalize their unhappiness and instead set out to change it.

When I think of "powerful" people, I think of two very good friends that I have known since high school. They both are fantastic musicians and are both very humble, they are quiet, but they possess immense ability to do 'things' in this world. They have always been a major source of inspiration for me both musically and as a model of how I wanted to be as a person. Because of the way that they make me feel, they support me and listen to me, for that I admire them because they temporarily put themselves aside to listen to me. This is respect.

Ironically one recently told me that I was a major inspiration to them. I had no idea. This surprised me because I had difficulty seeing it in myself; because I know that they are better than me in so many ways. But I suppose if we saw the "greatness" in ourselves then we would be arrogant and arrogance is the total opposite of "greatness".

A common quality of them is that they are very humble and they are always uplifting to be around. They rarely talk about themselves and always seem more interested in what I have to say, then telling me about what they have been doing. So again they act as a support structure for me to express my experiences on. It is never advised to be a blabber mouth, but communication is important in helping piece together all situations. When one stands strong and internalizes their thoughts they are the most secure, so with the reverse perception of Internalizing Your Thoughts, it's not really so much so as being totally silent, but just be aware of what you let escape the dimension of your lips. Once you say it, it's out there forever, so be careful what you say to people. Trust your friends if you have people to talk to who are judgmental, but don't dump your entire life story on the man at the post office.

This is how a Sage should act because this is a quality of being a true friend. A true friend is a servant in a time of need. A Sage listens to your story whole heartedly, never mind what they are thinking, they subjugate themselves for the needs of others. If someone needs help, they gladly offer a hand help.

Think for a moment, who is your servant? Who is always there for you? Some of you may be thinking Jesus. It is the Sage like characteristics that make Jesus and his teaching so powerful. Jesus is a prime example of how a Sage would conduct themselves. Jesus taught us to be a servant to other people; this is perhaps the most important character trait of a Sage, being a selfless servant, an unconditional servant to humanity. Think of the opposite, people that are self-absorbed. Those type of people are miserable to be around, and their insecurities push people away with a great force. It is because they have absolutely nothing to offer other people but endless hours of life draining attention demanding attention.

People like this are etheric vampires that feed off your energy to remain alive. I mean this is the most literal and real sense. It's true, you know it is, but I don't believe it is out of malice or Evil. It's mostly out of ignorance and not knowing how to control themselves. It may be because they are so out of touch with other people's feelings they are unaware of reality. It's sad really because there isn't much you can do for them except to be the Sage; subjugate your own ego and listen to them. You can't tell them how they need to change because they won't listen and it's not really our place to go around trying to change people. Instead all that we can do is allow them to feed off what we have to offer, our time, love and attention.

The Etheric Vampire, ha-ha at least it's not a zombie.

The vampire's heart has grown cold and dark from a lack of love and affection over the years. Years of neglect will do strange things to people. It's sad from an emotional stand point, but if you step outside of the emotion you will see the raw truth. A vampire only exists out of hardheadedness and ignorance. In the end it is no one's fault but their own, yes perhaps they were not taught how to act or love as a child, but that excuse only lasts through childhood. In the adult life we must accept responsibility for our own actions. We are adults. We are mature. Therefore we must accept total responsibility for our life. Accepting responsibility is obtaining true power. The vampire is so concerned about themselves they suck on others until they are depleted and must flee away. But a Sage is strong and offers hope and inspiration.

Moving back to one of my sources of inspiration is not only one of the best musicians that I know, but he is also one of the most physically fit people I know. It is the complete and total mastery that makes him so inspirational, the total opposite of a vampire. People like controlled strength; it makes them feel secure and safe. To give you an example of how talented my friend is, when we were 16 years old he was literally playing Van Halen's Eruption guitar solo with his guitar held behind his head. To top it off I remember our junior year he could bench press 325 pounds. So to reiterate the importance of discipline and self-control, you can never have enough of either.

A Sage quietly expresses total control over themselves and their lives. They do this by Will Power; the magick that permits you mastery over your life. Have you ever tried desperately to achieve something, only to find you have pushed your goal further away? Say there is a man or a woman you find yourself attracted to and in your pursuit he or she felt uncomfortable and retreated? This is a very simple process and it happens all too often to many people, it is basically caused by a lack of finesse and awareness. The trick is to not try to do anything. The answer lies in attracting your goal to you. A sincerely beautiful woman does not "try" to go out and "find" a man. She simply puts herself in the right situation and lets the right man find her. Now she wouldn't find the right man sitting in her apartment crying because she's lonely now would she? It requires concerted action and effort on her part, but she does not struggle to make ends meet. She goes out, but does so at her leisure. This is because over the eons women have developed a beautiful power within themselves. It is a mysterious beauty that communicates value. Some men have it also, but because of our culture men find it more awkward to accept beauty, the ones that do smile often and have beautiful smiles. People can be desperate; desperation is the go to program for someone inexperienced and insecure. Desperation is an affirmation of lack and the ego's inefficient way to beg and cry until someone gives it what it wants. It's a method learned as a child that often carries over into our adult lives. However desperation acts as a metaphysical bug repellant that repels any ounce of success. In the inner worlds desperation is a power energy vampires use to gain power. The wispy etheric arms of the vampire's etheric reaches out and wraps around the healthy etheric of the victim, and sucks the life away until the victim is close to death or until they become a vampire of their own. At which point the vampire can't feed anymore because the victim has become one of them or runs away. It all sounds so hocus pocus, but it's very real and dark. I haven't decided if it is necessarily evil or if it's solely because of ignorance and a lack of true power. In the external physical reality desperation screams "Warning! Warning! This person is emotionally unstable and likely to explode at any moment! Distance yourself! Distance yourself! This person is dangerous and unsafe!" Be the controlled beautiful woman. Even if you are a man, be the controlled beauty. Be valuable. Don't be the common dirt clod that is found everywhere. Be the pristine diamond that everyone seeks. This takes work and concerted action. It can't be done simply by the thought alone. You have to get up and work towards your goal. Find inspiration from within. Your Higher Self is waiting there waiting to be discovered. The entire power of the universe is available to you, but you must find it from within. The God-Force is impartial if you do or don't take action, but once you have a glimpse of the world's available from within you will begin to understand how infinity really feels. You do have the power within. Internalize your life and work on your Will Power and the magick of life will be revealed. Now let's continue on to talking about being a diamond.

The Seed of Life

Three creates all things.

The Flower of Life

Chapter 6:

The Discipline of the Diamond

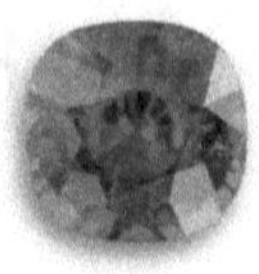

The Discipline of the Diamond

A good product does not need marketing and hype, it sells itself, because it has real value. Our goal as "Diamonds" is to basically be a valuable person who is desirable, of high quality, pure, and rare. The alternative to a diamond is a dirt clod, all ground is sacred, but when you have the choice to be dirt or a gemstone, which do you pick? One is common and walked on while the other is admired for its natural beauty. You have that natural beauty, we all have it, some might have flaws, and others might be scratched, scarred, and imperfect. But with some work and a little polish, you can be cleaned up nicely to have your real value shine. But "Diamonds" are not made over night.

Think of this, what is value? What does it take to make something truly valuable? The list can be very extensive, but it generally falls in two basic categories being rare and useful. So

Be useful, be of high quality, and many life problems can be sidestepped. (this is all BS btw)

Chapter 7:

Discipline of Ditching Drag

The Universe functions in a way that nearly everything is designed to hold us back. Gravity holds us in orbit around the sun and sticking to the Earth, a lack of money might keep ya in the ghetto, and one too many fat cells keeps me a single man! Okay, okay, that is probably an offbeat joke, but it is to prove a point. Some of the things that hold us back are placed in the way by a thought, ditch the thought problem gone, or even better yet, control my diet and exercise. And grow healthier in the process.

Ditching things that hold us back can be difficult especially if that "something" is a relationship. It can be hard to let go of people, but if you know deep down that something isn't right, there is no point in trying to force it, as it will just cause further hardship down the road. This is true with jobs, friends, debt, and sometimes even family members. While it is best to usually not cut off your roots of your family tree, sometimes this is necessary to leave a situation that is not beneficial spiritually, physically, mentally, emotionally, and even financially.

"Be free enough to say 'no' and do not be afraid to walk away from anything that does not contribute to your overall wellbeing, freedom, and happiness."

Chapter 8:

The Discipline of Silence.

Chapter 9:

The Discipline of Diet

The Discipline of Diet

Earlier I mentioned the importance of **Thought – Word – Action**, this literally ties into everything including the management of one's thoughts and desires for hunger. Humans can be pretty disturbing and over consumption is more ghoulish than we might like to really admit, I know, I am guilty of it myself, slopping down a triple quarter pounder with cheese, bacon, and top it off with hot-sauce. So we all know the driving power of hunger and consumption. All that needs to be said in this chapter is:

Junk in, Junk Out

Control Consumption

Eat Less

Hungry…

Chapter 10:

Discipline of Intellect

The Discipline of Itellenct

This is something our society focuses on to the extreme. We are taught in school to not act up, obey the rules, do things the way they are supposed to be done, and always make a better grade than everyone else, especially the Chinese kid. "I can't let the Chinese girl beat me on the accounting final, I mean she's over here not even speaking her native language and I let her win?... Come on bro. That's weak. Well... It is math after all, kinda... I mean, there's words there too. Egh, whatever. I'll let her win this time, but wait until I get my art degree."

University, it was fun. Business School, eh, it's alright. Not much room for creativity though, during my last semester I told em' I was writing a book, I even gave a final sales presentation in a marketing class about this book. They thought I was joking. I said: Do I look like the kind of person who would joke? But yeah, it was good fun. They had no idea who I really am, I tried to show them how to step out of this dimension into another via the humming of my singing bowl. They didn't get it, or maybe they did. I'll never know. I showed up to class the first group day wearing a flaming clown hat, I still have difficulty why they couldn't take me serious. Maybe they only see with their eyes? I don't know, college is interesting – it promotes "freedom of thought" but when you say things that are against what the professor wants to hear, you fail philosophy. I never failed, I knew what my professor wanted to hear, the only thing was, was I was too stupid to not tell him the truth. I cared about that GPA. GPA's are mostly bullshit anyway. It's good to know things and to study and commit yourself to getting an education or something equivalent. Hell I don't care what you do, just don't bother me. But, it's not a competition.

The really competitive education programs, they are really funny. I wouldn't know, I ran from all of the structure after graduation, I'm still running. Student loans? Yea that's another trap for the ignorant 18 year old who don't have the slightest idea about compound interest, shoulda got a business degree. Oh wait they don't teach that until your all in. But yeah, the really competitive programs make me laugh, competition in general makes me laugh. A lawyer once told me that their law school was so competitive that for the week of final exams a guy went and hid all of the books in the library ceiling tiles. That's why I say competition is funny - because it's not rational. I could understand if it were a fried chicken leg or slice of bologna, but a book, no way. Books are only good for reading and that's it, burning if you get lost in the Antarctic.

Burn this book if you get lost, please don't try to eat it.

But yeah, intellectual discipline, it's good, but don't take it too serious it's mostly competition like I said, and when "they" come, you can't eat a book remember.

Eat – Eat – Eat – More – More – More.

That's what consumption does to people, it makes them fat. I suppose the right word fathead is right, you know the ones? The posters?

But seriously, what good does it serve? Oh yeah, it's fun? Yay! You win! Congrats! Here is one more GPA point for you! Spend it wisely Ole' sport!

Sports, they also make me laugh. I'm not better than sports, but sports are just mostly a waste of time, more barbed wire from the matrix. Maybe you will be able to plow through them when they get here, but good luck, probably not. You would be better off throwing a book at em'.

But enough of that. Let's have a laugh, shall we?

Chapter 11:

Discipline of Laughter

Chapter 12:

Discipline of Acceptance

The Discipline of Acceptance

This can be a tough one. Especially when it's your family members or other loved ones who make you pull your hair out. I got lucky, my family has good sense. It must be genetics or something, hell I don't know. I'm not a scientist, but I do know this: just think of em' as God's gift of teaching you how not to be an asshole like them. We already know we can't change others with words alone, actions speaks louder than words, but even still people are going to do what they want to do. So go ahead and let go of trying to force things to change. It is pointless to try with words to change someone who won't listen anyway. Sometimes a good ole' sock in the nose is what they are really asking for. And sometimes it's good to punch em'. They will accept it and say "received sir, good morning sir!"

But yea, don't drive yourself crazy attempting to "save" someone, let them take care of themselves, love them, accept them. That's all we can do, really. Do this and you will be happier and probably live longer, assuming you don't own a pit bull. I've watched the news, those dogs eat people, I heard a story of one in Las Vegas, and it has done all sorts of nasty things, probably even carries a gun. But yeah, vicious animals, they certainly shouldn't be allowed to carry a weapon.

But like most dogs, you can teach it to sit, stay, roll over, but there's going to come a point in its life when it's going to shit or piss on the cashmere carpet. Accept it, it's not real cashmere anyway, it's actually camels hair. Thank God it wasn't real cashmere, if it were you would have been forced to take the dog out back and shoot it, but watch out. It might have a gun and shoot you right back. Then you'd be dead. So it's easier just to accept things and not worry about it. It's also best to not need a cashmere carpet. Hell, why even need carpet at all? It would be a quicker clean up.

But yeah, just try to not be an asshole. Be accepting of others and all of their stupidity, you can love people if you can, some people can't love themselves, so they are screwed from the get go, it's also nice to be forgiving, thankful, and etc.

"But no matter what is on your plate, be grateful."

~Nahko Bear & Medicine for the People

Chapter 13:

Discipline of Truth

中孚

Inner Peace is Inner Truth, and that's the truth.

A harsh Reality

The truth will set you free, but is the truth the whole truth and nothing but the truth? No, not necessarily. Many people's moral truths are opinions. Most moral truth is culturally based opinions developed by the individual culture in order preserve a specific way of life. For example: Is it or is it not true if you were raised in Iraq your "true God" would probably be called Allah? Of course! Because religion is location based. The religion you were born into is the right one for you. Unless it's a lie. Lies aren't good, but people believe lies, they like to believe lies.

In Iraq and other Middle Eastern countries they are not allowed to hear the truths of other cultures. Cultures forcibly censor themselves out of their own ignorance and fear. We are all born completely ignorant and most things are taught to us by our peers. Most of it is cultural Matrix Programming, you never fully question until you leave the confines of your cultural influence. There has to be a gap, time, distance, and travel. Get out of there. The circle, it ain't the whole truth.

Humans are the only animals that rely on culture in order to survive. Humans are the most evolved animals on Earth and culture is used to pass on the evolutionary memory, also to collect the collective memory. The fact is many cultures prohibit their people from exploring outside their bubble of perception. This is not necessarily a bad thing; it is just a defense of the Tribal Group Ego. It was more useful in previous centuries for survival; they couldn't speak each other's languages and stuff. So you really couldn't tell who was going to be friendly or eat you. At this point the specific culture's Ego has taken on a life of its own. That's one reason clothing fads sweep the world so quickly, as the people evolve, social trends start and take on a life of their own - somewhere within the dimension of the Collective Trendy Conscious of the Teenage Mind.

There is even a dimension for the individual Group Consciousness; I believe there is a collective conscious for all things. The squirrel has a collective conscious; all whales have a collective conscious, and so on. There is a group consciousness for people and even for individual cultures. It isn't the scientific definition of life, but then again scientists define the most basic unit of life a cell. A virus makes decisions, attacks, and even mutates all on its own, but is not considered alive, but it is very much alive. So I released the scientific definition of life a long time ago, it is to ridged, and by now we know what happens to things that are ridged. They break.

It is a slow process for individual people to ditch their tribal beliefs and tradition, but as time goes on that is exactly what we gradually do as people. We hardly recognize it because we don't necessarily ditch then, but we change them to fit our current understanding and because of ignorance we assume this is the same tradition as it has always been. An example of this is people who say they are old school Christian or are very traditional. Yes, they may be traditional relative to their grandparent's traditions, but compared to the Puritan beliefs it's drastically different and compared to the medieval ages it's a totally different religion. We are afraid of change especially when we are told as a small child if we change we will go to Hell, the Devil with get us, God won't love us anymore, and many other manipulative techniques to keep you loyal. But it is all just fear preaching dogma. Your family may believe it, you may believe it, and the other people of your culture may believe it, but it doesn't necessarily make it true. The only reason I have this position is because I have visited 9 different countries to date, and they all have had a different religion with vastly different beliefs. So I have a hard time believing everyone in Ukraine is going to Hell, or that everyone in Iraq is an enemy of God, or everyone in Zimbabwe are infidels. The reason cultures have said these things in the past are because an opposing culture often meant the death of your way of life. It's the death of things that scares people and if we base our lives literally on a book that was wrote 2,000 years ago conflict will occur. Because now it isn't life or death if a Muslim moves next door - we are no longer an immediate threat the way we once were especially when decisions were made by Kings, Queens, and people with building an Empire on their minds. We as the common person simply gets stuck in between and since our family members and culture is too afraid to let go of the fear preaching dogma we are raised believing literally everything is a sin and will make a seemingly immature God hate us for looking at our private parts. A book as this is hard to read for many people because it challenges everything you have been taught as a child. So it has the potential to put you on the defense trying to justify your views. I mean no harm and I am not implying I am the smarter and only I know better. Because I don't. All I know is I have a very hard time believing God is a manlike entity that gets pissed off if a woman doesn't wear her shemagh when she goes in public. There are some cultures in Africa that still remove the woman's clitoris because they believe it makes sex to pleasurable and will make her be faithful to her husband. I don't know about you, but I would almost guarantee it was a male that made this rule. Not very many woman would will fully have their clit removed, but when you have it in culture and your mom had it done, your sister had it done, and it's been going on and is written down in your holy book it suddenly transforms into a sacred ritual that cannot be questioned because it has now been written as law into the collective Ego of the collective conscious of the tribe. Now you may be thinking "but hey my religion doesn't do any of that crazy crap, we are civilized." Your religion very well may be very civilized which most Christians are more civilized compared to native tribes and even Muslims. But my purpose is to entice people to question what they believe in and really analyze if all of what they believe is true. Traditionally most people were totally forbidden to question, analyze, or even think about their religious beliefs because it was all determined for them by the state. This was very common when a country was conquered because the state leader has his or her own opinions and declared a state religion. This created the extinction of countless smaller religions and cultures especially tribal and native peoples. The tribal people probably believed some ridiculous things, but that is irrelevant because the ones conquering and exterminating believe equally ridiculous stuff, the difference is they had power, resources, and most importantly, control. So let's kill all of the soulless savaged and the ones that survive we will convert to the state religion. Great idea... They justified their moves because they believed they were somehow better and more special and they were Gods people, when in reality they were just self-absorbed ego driven people scared of the uncertainty of life. So they created these belief systems in order to justify their actions. We are still doing this today. A good example of this is with Christian churches that are now beginning to bend and accept homosexuals into their congregation, when just a century ago they would imprison them, kill them, or who knows what else because they are an abomination anyway and God hates them. The liberal churches that are allowing homosexuals are starting to see something just isn't right about all of this. There is a lot of debate whether people are born gay or whatever, but obviously people are born gay. Being homosexual is obviously not a choice, what person would choose to be someone that will be exiled, ridiculed, and hated upon? Instead it's a malicious virus of the mind. It is designed to kill people and spread venereal disease. It's a malicious brain virus that "gay" people believe that they "can't resist." They can, anyone can resist anything. If you want too, that is. Sorry, I don't mean to be rude, judgmental, or anything, but don't believe the lies, everything is a choice, to be gay, straight, to be attracted to a child, it's not the "thought" that's so bad. It's the action. This includes sex with the opposite sex, sex isn't bad, it's the risk that's bad, that's all I am saying. Its risky business and anyone who acts like it's not has obviously never had an STD. STD's are a good way to make people mature, some are hard as hell to get rid of. Some are just little warning signs that say "hey dude, you better be more responsible." Others say: "You're fucked, I'm going to kill you, slowly." Then they kill you.

Then people argue and say "God would never make someone be born gay." Nah he wouldn't, but I'll tell you what, mutations are a part of reality, remember the STD's? Those are mutations. Same logic would say "God would never give me a genetic mutation!" Nah he wouldn't, but you being an idiot screwing around like an irresponsible teenager will give you mutations. Is gay a mutation? Nah, but people born with both genitalia are. God gives that to them, I don't know why, "shit happens. I guess."

But yeah, there are viruses everywhere, we have skin for a reason, to protect our bodies, so just be careful what you let penetrate you or vice versa. Will you go to hell for being gay? Nah, but will you be exposing yourself to a greater risk? I don't know. You tell me. You have the choice to be safe, smart, or stupid - both gays and straight people. Transsexuals on the other hand, they are just asking for it, (no pun intended.) Seriously though, that is just asking to invite abuse into your life. Many transsexual women, that means they are a man under the disguise of a woman, yeah. They get killed pretty often, it's in the newspapers and such, TV don't report it because it's "offensive." I suppose you could be transsexual and still survive, but if you don't come right out and tell someone you have a dick, I'm telling you, you're just putting yourself into a vulnerable position. But that's what the whole agenda is, is to have someone "dominate" you. It's the truth; you can deny it if you want, but that's all that the TV promoted sex and pornographic sex is - various forms of exposing of people and domination. It's not right, wanking off 5 times on your computer screen before you go into work is not normal. And then to go in to the office and say "Hello Tom, beautiful weather were having today, have we received the package for the Peter's order?" Then you shake their hand pretending that you're a normal person. Comon', now, be honest with yourself. The porn sites even have "Evil" branded into their marketing. I know, because I'm not perfect; but you can escape from it and find a healthy relationship. You just need to create an action plan for weaning off the programmed addiction; its corrupt, sexual power over people is an easy way to get what you want. Being a transsexual woman is an easier way to entice another man to have sex with you. I've met one before, I offended him when I asked what made him want to be a girl while guy friends wanted to stay a man. I was asking an honest question, the gay guy told me the truth, he said "I just identify as being a man." The trans girl, he got offended and walked away. He asked me what I was doing at a bar alone, it wasn't a gay bar either. I looked him right in the eye and asked if he was a tranny. He said yea, that's when I asked why? Offensive I know, but I'm just telling the truth. I'm just thankful that he wasn't attractive. I'm kidding, but seriously that's why they trans, like it or not, that is the only reason. They want to be more convincing so guys will have sex with them.

So yeah, there you have it. Be careful what you get exposed too. Once you see, you can't unsee, once you hear, you can't unhear. There's an old Chinese story with three little monkeys. For them to be monkeys they are pretty wise, most monkeys are stupid and throw shit at you, these are smart. They say hear no evil, see no evil, speak no evil. See pretty damn smart to be a monkey. If we evolved from monkeys it sure weren't them three, they are actually symbols for the Hindu Monkey God Hanuman. That's the God of Strength, Perseverance and Devotion. It's real. But yeah, I'm telling you, unplug from the porn sites. Here's what you can do if you feel that you can't stop. Go buy a ring and wear it on your porn watching hand, empower the ring with the wisdom of those monkeys. In order to do your business you will have to take the ring off, like cheating on your spouse in order to cheat yourself you must remove the ring. The ring will work. The monkeys will help you, we did evolve from them after all.

Masturbation isn't the problem; the lack of self-control is the problem. That and you are contributing to funding the porn sites that expose and dominate people, it's nasty. They get paid ad revenue, so you are guilty and a part of the system just by watching.

The only way out is by total removal. If you want to masturbate try doing it to something other than a porno. You will see… It's a little harder, you know why? You know why. They got a grip on you and they say "you are powerless and can't let go." You can, you have loads of power.

So…

Flip em' the bird and tell them you have Monkey Brains,

they won't like that but at least you will be free.

Chapter 14:

Discipline of Leadership

Welcome to The End, congratulations. I'd say many folks didn't make it here, that's okay. We can wave them goodbye another day. But hey, I saved the best for last. Here it is.

As you develop and expand your influence in this world people may start to look up to you. This is pretty much switching from being a part of the wave to becoming a particle. So in the particle state you have quite a bit of responsibility, you better represent yourself to the best, because this is what teaches others how to be. Then once your lessons have been taught, you can join back with the wave, disappear, like camouflage, no one will be observing you any longer. This could be due to death, loss of status, or maybe you have just taught all that you need to teach, so you slip out of this dimension, step sideways, away, back into the safety of the wave. The wave is a good place to be, it's safe. Nobody knows your there, like a Wilde animal — you see the people running amuck, busy, frantic, tick-tocking looking for a way out. They are too busy, they don't see you. The wave is the natural state of all of physical reality, the particle state is mostly an imbalance, an imbalance based on the need of observation, leaders are particles, they get assassinated sometimes too, the wave get's em.

Animals, they don't want to be seen, they are smarter than humans. Humans are stupid. Animals hide because they know of the eating ceremonies that the humans participate in, zombies, I'm telling you. When the delivery trucks stop delivering, people will eat, they will eat anything. You know it's true. What did you eat today? I bet it came from a store of some type. So now you can see why the wave is safe, the particle state is uncertain, unstable.

In the particle state you are a leader, little kids, they will look up at you. Especially if you are a particle on the television, I've been that before, it's weird, it still amazes me how I can be everywhere at once, a wave in a wire someplace, and then popped into the particle state on a TV screen. When you pop on a big screen, little screen, or even just walking down the sidewalk, you better remember one thing. This is the real lesson of this book. Forget most of the other garbage; it's mostly barbed wire for the mind anyway. So you better be something that will be good for them to look at. I think that's all that should be said about leadership, if you must be a particle:

"Be a worthy particle and watch out for the Zombies, they are coming."

Good Luck,

AJ

First Writing,

Easter Sunday

March 31, 2013

OTHER TAIJITU HOUSE TITLES

Books

The Children of R, by 1.3.0

The Search for the Hidden Door, Marshall N. Lever

We hope you enjoyed this *Taijitu House* book. For more information on authors, titles, and author events please visit our website at:

WWW.TAIJITUHOUSE.COM

The Two Dimensional Realities:

One Will Become True

Two Dimensional Realities: One Will Become True

There are two probabilities that will likely come to pass in the not so distant future. How long exactly, it is hard to tell. But I assure you, one of these events will come to pass, it is our responsibility to educate people of the "likely hoods". Previous civilizations have gone through these already. It is in the subconscious minds of popular culture, we have a feeling something is coming but do not know exactly what.

Well these are the two options and I literally mean only two options. The Great Collapse or The Great Expansion; either one will have serious consequences and the world needs to be made aware of the probabilities and likelihoods, immediately. Because at the rate that we are currently expanding, consuming, destroying, and standing by passively without taking action, the closer we come to the less desirable option. Either one could happen and very quickly. Who knows how long, months, years, decades, or maybe even in a century or more, but either way civilizations have come, grown, reached their cap and ultimately collapsed. So what is the big deal? Well in our closely quartered and heavily populated society, people will have no clue on how to survive. But I assure you, they will find a way, and they will eat. What they will eat? Anything that they can.

1.) **The Great Expansion:** This is the happier option. However, based on history and the current outlook, perhaps the least likely. This would require complete and total cooperation, selflessness, and a forfeiture of greed by all governments, religions, and peoples. If balance can be achieved, then will continue to expand exponentially like we have been doing the past 100 years; we will finally begin using free energy technology that will enable humans to focus more resources on food production, farming, and stop depleting the natural resources of the planet. And then sometime in the future we will expand on to other planets - therefore solving the finite resource problem caused by Earth being a closed looped system. Meaning if we cut down all the trees and pour concrete all over the place, where will we get food from? So if we can control our consumption and actually utilize the free energy technology that IS available, the expansion would happen and we would be OK. This is the best option, but not very likely, greed is the main problem. We have free energy available today, it's called the sun. The sun powers all life on Earth, it could power our homes, cars, and everything else for a fraction of the cost, but that would be at the loss of profits of the Oil and Power Industries. Is this possible? Yes, is it probable? Not at the rate we are going. The graph below is of an exponential function, more specifically an e^x function between time and population. As one can assume, it has an inverse based on food and resources. More people more food needed. Its dependent on supply and demand

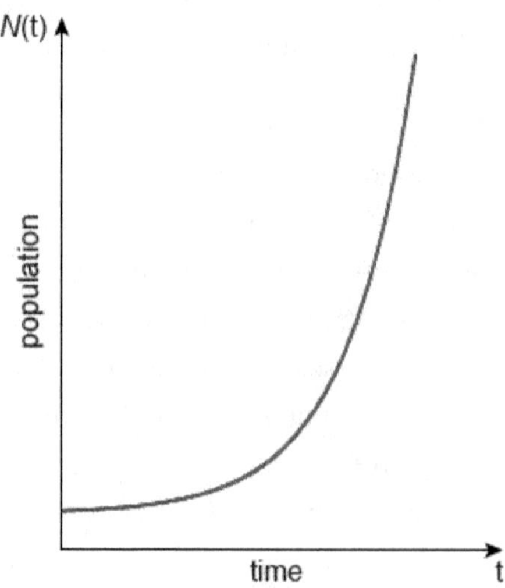

2.) **The Great Collapse:** In this dimensional reality Human society is unable to solve the limited resource problem caused by human consumption. We continue to consume at the normal rate and continue further expansion until our food supply is completely exhausted, the distribution systems fail, and the super markets no longer have food. People will NOT go hungry and people will NOT starve to death. We can see that right now, yes some people will starve to death, but it will not be long before zombies walk the Earth. Not zombies like seen on TV. We are talking about humans who will do anything in order to survive. We are talking about intentional murder turned to cannibalism. It has happened before and it WILL happen again one day in the distant or maybe not so distant future. It is already manifesting in the subconscious minds of the public in popular culture, TV, video games, art, literature, and etc. I am not certain how many people have heard the message but it is being said pretty loud and clear, these movies, video games, and TV series such as The Walking Dead, they are not just entertainment, they are unintentional education programs showing the world, what would happen if society collapsed. The idea of a walking dead is not a new idea. Instead of being physically dead, they would be dead without a soul, resorting to cannibalism in order to survive.

April 5th 2015. Happy Easter!

THE END

Bibliography

1.3.0. Ranald. The Children of R. Johnson City, TN: Taijitu House, 2015. Print

Bravandt, Deborah. Free Your Mind: Unplug from the Matrix. http://thetruthawaits.com/1/post/2014/10/free-your-mind-unplug-from-the-matrix-by-deborah-bravandt.html

Cross, Spenser. The Great Pyramid: A Factory for Mono-Atomic Gold. Spencer L. Cross. November 15, 2013. Print.

Chung Fu. Under the Plum Tree. Inkwell; 3rd Updated edition September 1, 2010. Print.

Cunningham, Jason. Approaching Singularity: The Genesis of Creation. Reinhardt & Still Publishers. 2012. Print.

Crowely, Aliester. 777 And Other Qabalistic Writings of Aleister Crowley: Including Gematria & Sepher Sephiroth. Indianapolis, IN: Weiser Books, 1986. Print

Kings James Bible, Oxford, (1796)

King, Stephen. The Jaunt. The Twilight Zone Magazine. 1983. Print.

Lever, Marshall. The Search for the Hidden Door. Melbourne, Australia. Brolga Publishing Pty Ltd, 1981. Print.

Plato. The Allegory of the Cave. http://faculty.washington.edu/smcohen/320/cave.htm

Spalding, Geof. The 33rd Sage and the Initiate. Indianapolis, IN: Dog Ear Publishing, 2012. Print.

Spalding, Geof. The 33rd Sage: A Modern Fable. Indianapolis, IN: Dog Ear Publishing, 2011. Print.

Spalding, Geof. The Way of the Initiate: Legend of the 33rd Sage. Indianapolis, IN: Dog Ear Publishing, 2014. Print.

The Suicide of Socrates. Eye Witness History. http://www.eyewitnesstohistory.com/socrates.htm

Wilde, Stuart. God's Gladiator's. Carlsbad, CA: Brooke Mark LLC, 2003. Print.

Wilde, Stuart. Infinite Self. Carlsbad, CA: Hay House, 1996. Print.

Wilde, Stuart. Life Was Never Meant to be a Struggle. Carlsbad, CA: Hay House, 1998. Print.

Wilde, Stuart. Little Money Bible: The Ten Laws of Abundance. Carlsbad, CA: Hay House, 2001. Print.

Wilde, Stuart. Plum Red: Taoist Tales of Old China. Tolemac, 2011. Print

Wilde, Stuart. Silent Power. Carlsbad, CA: Hay House, 2005. Print.

Wilde, Stuart. Sixth Sense: Including the Secrets of the Etheric Subtle Body. Carlsbad, CA: Hay House, 2000. Print.

Wilde, Stuart. The Force. Carlsbad, CA: Hay House, 2003. Print.

Wilde, Stuart. The Quickening. Carlsbad, CA: Hay House, 1995. Print.

Wilde, Stuart. The Trick to Money is Having Some. Carlsbad, CA: Hay House, 1995. Print.

Wilde, Stuart. Weight Loss for the Mind. Carlsbad, CA: Hay House, 1998. Print.

Wilde, Stuart. Whispering Winds of Change. Carlsbad, CA: Hay House, 1983. Print.

www.ingramcontent.com/pod-product-compliance
Lightning Source LLC
Chambersburg PA
CBHW060023100426
42740CB00010B/1575